A CALL TO HOPE

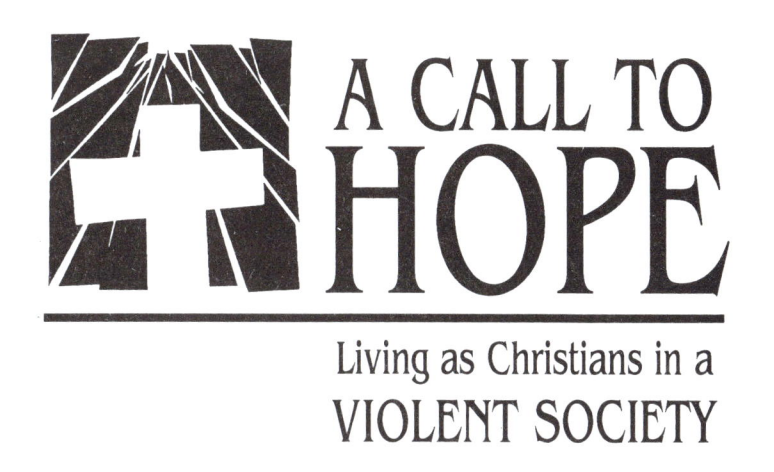

Living as Christians in a VIOLENT SOCIETY

Vera K. White

Friendship Press • New York

To Alex and Adam
because I pray that your world will be secure and peaceful

Copyright © 1997 by Friendship Press
ISBN 377–00311–5

Editorial Offices:
475 Riverside Drive, Room 860, New York, NY 10115–0050
Distribution Offices:
PO Box 37844, Cincinnati, OH 45222–0844

Unless otherwise indicated Bible quotations are from the New Revised Standard Version, copyright © 1989 by the Division of Christian Education of the National Council of the Churches of Christ in the U.S.A. Used by permission.

All rights reserved. No part of this publication may be reproduced, stored in a retrieval system, or transmitted in any form or by any means, electronic, mechanical, photocopying, recording, or otherwise, without the prior permission of the copyright owner, except for brief quotations included in a review of the book or within restrictions as follows: Pages 24 and 63 may be copied for one-time group use during the study.

Library of Congress Cataloging-in-Publication Data
White, Vera K.
 A call to hope : living as Christians in a violent society / Vera K. White.
  p. cm.
 Includes bibliographical refrences.
 ISBN 0-377-00311-5
 1. Violence—Religious aspects—Christianity. 2. Violence—United States.   3. United States—Social conditions—1980–   4. United States—Moral conditions. I. Title
BT736.15.W485 1997
241'.697—dc21   96–48265
                                                        CIP

Manufactured in the United States of America.

Contents

Introduction 5

ONE: Violence: A Christian Response .9

TWO: Power Structures and Justice 19

THREE: Violence, Children, and Youth 31

FOUR: Thorns of Pain and Fear: Domestic Violence 45

FIVE: Violence in the Media 55

SIX: Faith as Hope, Faith as Mandate 63

Resources 77

      Worship Resources 78

      Study Resources 82

      Organizations 88

      Videography 90

Endnotes 95

Introduction

We live our lives in the shadow of violence. Violence stalks our paths, follows us into the sanctity of our homes, and threatens the security of our existence. The carefully woven cloth of our modern world is unraveling before our eyes. The threat of violence haunts our lives and our daily activities.

How are Christians called to respond to the violence of our world? How can we stand beside the victims, offer healing to the perpetrators, and bring a message of hope to a society that is in despair?

God offers words of hope and power for a new way of living. Followers of Christ bring light and peace into a world filled with darkness and fear.

The causes of violence are complex and varied, and there is no quick fix. Sociologists point to poverty and racial or ethnic tensions as some root causes. The glorification of violence in the mass media helps to create a climate where violence seems an appropriate response to social evils. The easy availability of lethal weapons compounds the seriousness of the problem. Much of society's violence can be tracked to drug trafficking. Seeds of violence are planted in homes where abusive behavior and aggression are the norm. There may be almost as many causes for violence as there are acts of violence.

Work to end violence must take place on many levels and in many venues: schools, families, government, medical care facilities, neighborhoods, and churches, among others. Violence in our society is, at its core, a spiritual problem. Perhaps it is the church that is best qualified to make a difference.

NOTES TO LEADER

We live in a society where violence is a way of life. Some members of your group may have experienced physical abuse or live in homes where violence is an acceptable way of handling problems. The themes of this resource may allow people to recall painful experiences. Someone in the group may become aware through your discussions that a loved one or family member is a victim of abuse. Participants may even seek help in controlling their own violent natures. As a leader you may find yourself in the position of confidant. Sometimes victims and perpetrators of violence long for help but don't know where to turn. They appreciate knowing that someone cares and is willing to listen. It is a big responsibility to be a friend to a person in crisis. You need to know where to find appropriate help if you need it.

Before leading this study, you will want to have certain information available. Support agencies vary from community to community. Help is available from a variety of sources: schools, religious organizations, medical facilities, government agencies, and private organizations. The following general guide to support services is designed to help you find the kind of help you may need within your own community.

WHERE TO TURN

1. Many pastors have up-to-date information on community services and family counselors.

2. Schools have nurses, counselors, and psychologists who are knowledgeable about child welfare laws and children and family services. Some schools have special programs designed to identify children at risk.

3. A physician can deal with physical injuries and also can help you find psychological treatment. Hospitals also have a variety of services for victims of abuse.

4. The Human Services section of your telephone book provides emergency telephone numbers to report abuse or to seek help for child abuse, domestic abuse, rape, suicide, drug or alcohol abuse, and other emergencies.

5. A Child Line is a toll-free number that can be used to report anonymously cases of physical or sexual abuse of children. All situations reported must be investigated. Check the Emergency or Human Services, or Social Service section in your phone book.

6. Child welfare agencies are included in the government listings in the telephone book.

7. The Yellow Pages has listings under Counseling Services, Domestic Violence, Abuse, and Family Services. Some agencies offer a sliding scale or can provide counseling for people who do not have the money to pay for it.

8. The United States has a national hotline for victims of domestic abuse. It provides information about shelters, legal advocacy, health care, and counseling twenty-four hours a day. The number is 1–800–799–SAFE (7233). A special number for the hearing impaired is 1–800–787–3224.

9. Some police departments receive special training in dealing with emergency calls related to domestic abuse. The police can be helpful in many kinds of emergency situations. Find out what services your local police department offers.

USING THIS BOOK

This resource contains six chapters. Each chapter can be used as a study session. The outline at the beginning of each chapter suggests a format for a one-hour session.

Use this resource for personal study, an adult or youth church school class, an ecumenical or interfaith discussion group, a community organization, or as the program for a weekend retreat. Pastors will find helps for planning sermons.

Each study session is self-contained. You may wish to use only selected sessions in which case you will want to be sure to include "Getting Started" and "Creating a Covenant" from Chapter 1 to begin the study. Suggestions for group leaders appear throughout the resource. If you are working with a group that enjoys discussion, the material may take longer than one hour to cover. Leaders will want to decide ahead of time which activities have priority. Leaders should feel free to adapt the material to suit their groups.

KEEPING A JOURNAL

One way of growing in your spiritual life is to keep a journal of your thoughts, experiences, prayers, and other ways that you feel God is speaking to you. Throughout this book are questions for reflection or discussion that may also provide you with ideas for journal writing.

CHAPTER ONE

Violence: A Christian Response

*God saw everything that God had made,
and indeed, it was very good.*

Gen. 1:31a

A WORD AT THE START

We have become intensely aware in recent years that we live in a world where violence reigns. Through television and movies we visit intimately scenes of war, riots, and murder that occur far away. Crimes of violence encroach on our own backyards and violate our safe neighborhoods. We have become a frightened people. We escape to suburbia, add deadbolts to our doors, train our pets to attack strangers, and suspect anyone who is different from us.

Yet throughout scripture God's people are admonished, "Be not afraid." Is this a message that still has relevance for Christians in North America as they look forward to the third millennium? What does God have to say to us about the culture in which we live? How can we be secure in God's protective love when we live in a world where violence is out of control?

Christians are an Easter people with a message of hope for the world. God's hope was not just for a small group of Jewish people living in a faraway corner of the world thousands of years ago but for all people of all times. The future of this world depends on people of faith and hope. We dare not sit back from the safety of our pews and watch our society self-destruct. We need to be "ambassadors of Christ" in our world today.

> A young man fleeing two pursuers with automatic weapons ducks into a church during a worship service, believing he will be safe there. His assailants don't even pause at the church door as they rush in and open fire. The choir stops singing, the preacher dives under the pulpit, and the congregation crouches beneath the pews as the sanctuary is sprayed with bullets.

Outline for a One-hour Study Session

Prepare for the Session
- Read "Introduction," "Notes to Leader," and "Using This Book."
- Read Chapter 1.

Begin the Session
- Introduce the study and Session 1.
- Lead "Getting Started."
- Lead "Creating a Covenant."

Develop the Session
- Ask a volunteer to read aloud "A Violent Society," and lead a group discussion using "Reflection or Discussion No. 1."
- Read "How Do Christians Respond to Violence," and lead a discussion using "Reflection or Discussion No. 4."
- Read "Forgiveness: A Biblical Perspective," and lead a discussion using "Reflection or Discussion No. 5."

Conclude the Session
- Use the "Closing" activities.

Later, at a press conference, church leaders indignantly decry the blasphemous violation of holy thresholds and sacred space. But Azusa Christian Community's Eugene Rivers, an African-American street pastor, offered a different and prophetic word: "If the church won't go into the streets, the streets will come into the church."[1]

How do we go out into the streets? This resource will help Christians explore how they can be ministers of God's word within a violent society.

Getting Started

If there are people in your group who do not know each other well, begin by having the group members introduce themselves.

Then have each person finish the following sentence: "When I think of violence, I . . ." If you are doing this study with a group, write the unfinished sentence on the chalkboard or a sheet of newsprint. Give members a minute of silence to think about their answers. Explain that it is acceptable to keep responses private, but encourage those who are willing to do so to give their responses aloud.

If you are reading this book by yourself, you may want to write your response in your journal. (See "Keeping a Journal," in the Introduction.)

Creating a Covenant

You are about to embark on a journey of discovery as you find out just how deeply violence has scarred our society. You may find this to be an uncomfortable journey, even frightening at times. It may be comforting to take some friends along for company as you set off on this trip. Why not use this study resource with a group in your church or community?

Each person has a story to tell. Your study group will allow you to tell your own story and to listen to the stories of others. However, no one said it would be easy! Sometimes recalling the past and telling our stories is a painful thing, especially for those who have been victims of violence, who have watched loved ones suffer, or who live lives of fear.

Create a covenant with the others in your group that will allow each person's story to be told in an atmosphere of trust and confidentiality.

Group Leaders: Write the provisions for the covenant on a piece of newsprint (see box). Ask whether any members of the group have any other provisions they would like to add. If there are any suggestions that meet the approval of the group, add them to the covenant. Seal your covenant by reading the prayer aloud together.

10 *Chapter One: Violence: A Christian Response*

Ask each participant in your group to agree to abide by the provisions of this covenant for as long as your group continues to meet together.

> Covenant
> 1. I will respect each person's right to privacy when we discuss painful or difficult subjects.
> 2. I will listen carefully, giving my full attention, as each person speaks. I will not interrupt or contradict.
> 3. I believe that each person is a child of God, worthy of my love and respect. I will treat each person in the group with respect.
> 4. I will share my own experiences as openly and honestly as I am able.

Prayer

O God of peace and justice, may we help to bring healing to a broken world. Help us to love each other well, to see your face in the faces of our neighbors, and to feel the pain of those who suffer. We pray that we might create a community of faith in this place. In the name of the Holy One, the Giver of Peace. Amen.

Reflection or Discussion No. 1

1. Recall silently your first experience (or an early experience) with violence as victim, offender, or witness. How did you feel when this event occurred? If you are doing this study as part of a group, you may choose to tell about your early memories of violence. *(Leaders, suggest that participants focus on the feelings that were associated with their experiences.)*

2. What is violence? Write down your personal responses to this question or if you are doing this study with a group, brainstorm aloud possible answers to the question with one volunteer writing the responses on a sheet of newsprint.

A Violent Society

What has caused the violence in our society to get out of control? Deborah Prothrow-Stith is a physician and assistant dean at Harvard School of Public Health. She is widely recognized as an authority on violence as a public health issue. Her book *Deadly Consequences: How Violence Is Destroying Our Teenage Population and a Plan to Begin Solving the Problem* examines contributing factors. In an interview for *Alive Now!* she discusses the causes of violence:

> I think there is a convergence of factors. It is like a slot machine where you have to get five oranges before you hit the jack-pot. One window is the widening gap of poverty over the last decade or so and the creation of an underclass. Another window includes alcohol use and other drugs. Another window is the increase in guns and their availability. Another window has to do with family problems and issues. Then I add one that I call our "make my day" ethic—the way we encourage and celebrate violence. You add all of that up and you've got an epidemic of youth violence. It's a complicated problem.[2]

Make My Day!

We can learn a lot about a society by listening. What do we hear when we listen to ourselves speak? Expressions of violence find their way into our everyday language: we attack problems, seize control, target solutions. We can "bomb a test" or "kill our opponent" in a chess match.

A mother of a young cheerleader from a Catholic high school recently returned from a cheerleading conference where she had spent the day listening to students from parochial schools perform their best cheers. She was astonished to hear chants such as: "Destroy Nativity High," "Massacre Holy Innocent," or "Kick some serious butt, Prince of Peace."

Make a list of some expressions of violence that make their way into our conversation. Look at the headlines in the sports section of your newspaper if you have trouble thinking of any. Compare your list with the others in your group.

What Does the Bible Say?

God saw everything that God had made, and indeed, it was very good. (Gen. 1:31a)

But now in Christ Jesus you who once were far off have been brought near by the blood of Christ. For he is our peace; in his flesh he has made both groups into one and has broken down the dividing wall, that is, the hostility between us. He has abolished the law with its commandments and ordinances, that he might create in himself one new humanity in place of the two, thus making peace, and might reconcile both groups to God in one body through the cross, thus putting to death that hostility through it. So he came and proclaimed peace to you who were far off and peace to those who were near; for through him both of us have access in one Spirit to the Father. So then you are no longer strangers and aliens, but you are citizens with the saints and also members of the household of God, built upon the foundation of the apostles and prophets, with Christ Jesus himself as the cornerstone. (Eph. 2:13–20)

For it was you who formed my inward parts;
    you knit me together in my mother's womb.
I praise you, for I am fearfully and wonderfully made.
    Wonderful are your works;
that I know very well.
    My frame was not hidden from you,
when I was being made in secret,
    intricately woven in the depths of the earth.
Your eyes beheld my unformed substance.
In your book were written
    all the days that were formed for me,
    when none of them as yet existed.
How weighty to me are your thoughts, O God!
    How vast is the sum of them! (Ps. 139:13–17)

What Is Violence?

The dictionary offers us some help in understanding violence. Among other definitions for "violate," we find the following:

- to break, infringe, or transgress
- to rape or ravish
- to treat without reverence
- to break in upon, disturb
- to offend, insult, outrage
- to treat roughly or abusively
- to desecrate, dishonor, or defile

Scripture helps us further in our understanding of violence. The violent nature of humanity has incurred God's judgment from the very beginning. God said to Noah, "I have determined to make an end of all flesh, for the earth is filled with violence because of them; now I am going to destroy them along with the earth" (Gen. 6:13).

Reflection or Discussion No. 2

1. What do these scripture passages tell us about the world that God created?
2. What do they communicate about God's plans for human relationships?

ACTIVITIES

1. Define:
   Look in a dictionary for the definitions and word derivations for *violence* and *violate*. You may use an unabridged dictionary if you have one; but for the most recent information, use an abridged dictionary, but check the copyright date for the most current edition.

2. Discuss:
   - What did you discover in your research and in the information given in the article "What is Violence?" that helps you to understand the meaning and the nature of *violence*?
   - What are the dangers to your nation and the world if people continue in their violent ways?

3. Write:
   Based on the dictionary definitions and scriptural guidelines, create your own individual or group definition of violence. Write this definition on newsprint and post it in your meeting room as you continue this study of violence.

The exile was God's response to a nation filled with violence:

I will avert my face from them, . . .
For the land is full of bloody crimes;
   the city is full of violence.
I will bring the worst of the nations
   to take possession of their houses. (Ezek. 7:22–24)

God promises that those who live violent lives will face appropriate consequences: "Their mischief returns upon their own heads, and on their own heads their violence descends" (Ps. 7:16).

The violence of the wicked will sweep them away,
   because they refuse to do what is just. (Prov. 21:7)

Jesus himself warned: "All who take the sword will perish by the sword" (Matt. 26:52).

God offers to those who will listen a vision for a different way of relating:

For I am about to create new heavens
   and a new earth; the former things shall not be remembered
   or come to mind. . . . The wolf and the lamb shall feed together.
They shall not hurt or destroy
   on all my holy mountain, says the LORD. (Isa. 65:17, 25a, d)

Is It for Real?

Is there a crime panic going on in Canada and the United States today? There seems to be some evidence that the *crime rates* have not risen nearly as much as the *public fear* of crime. A report from Toronto shows that the public perception is enhanced by media hype, political manipulation, and increased reporting of crimes by victims. New York City's crime rate has dropped dramatically to its lowest level in twenty-five years. In the first half of 1995, there appeared to be a 30 percent drop in murder and shooting incidents. The United States as a whole has been seeing less crime despite the fact that some cities continue to see crime rates on the rise.[3]

Does this indicate that the problem of violence is behind us? Are we fearful without reason? The trend is encouraging. While sociologists and criminologists continue to debate the meaning of the statistics, we must not let them lull us into a false sense of security. The United States is still one of the most violent nations on the face of the earth. Although crime rates in Canada are far lower than in the United States, some Canadian cities have felt the influence of their southern neighbors as they have witnessed several startling violent crimes in recent years.

How Do Christians Respond to Violence?

Nathan said to David, "You are the man! Thus says the LORD, the God of Israel: I anointed you king over Israel, and I rescued you from the hand of Saul; I gave you your master's house, and your master's wives into your bosom, and gave you the house of Israel and of Judah; and if that had been too little, I would have added as much more. Why have you despised the word of the LORD, to do what is evil in his sight? You have struck down Uriah the Hittite with the sword, and have taken his wife to be your wife, and have killed him with the sword of the Ammonites. Now therefore the sword shall never depart from your house, for you have despised me, and have taken the wife of Uriah the Hittite to be your wife." (2 Sam. 12:7–10)

Pilate then called together the chief priests, the leaders, and the people, and said to them, "You brought me this man as one who was perverting the people; and here I have examined him in your presence and have not found this man guilty of any of your charges against him. . . . he has done nothing to deserve death. I will therefore have him flogged and release him."

Then they all shouted out together, "Away with this fellow!" . . . "Crucify, crucify him!" . . .

When they came to the place that is called The Skull, they crucified Jesus there with the criminals, one on his right and one on his left. Then Jesus said, "Father, forgive them; for they do not know what they are doing." (Luke 23:13, 15b, 16, 18, 21, 33, 34)

The Bible is not filled with the sunny pictures of green pastures, stained-glass windows, and rainbows that we remember from Sunday school classes. In fact, if made into a realistic Hollywood movie, it might receive an R rating for its violent scenes. The Bible is loaded with stories of rape, pillage, the slaughter of babies, war, and stonings. It provides an uncensored picture of a broken humanity. Surely it must also provide some direction for a faithful response to violence.

Two well-known passages offer insight. The first appears in 2 Samuel, chapters 11 and 12. You might want to read the entire story to remind yourself of the events of King David's rape of Bathsheba and his consequent plan for the murder of her husband, Uriah.

This is David—the greatest king Israel ever knew, the model of faithfulness—guilty of rape, adultery, betrayal, shirking of responsibility, and ultimately of murder. In 2 Samuel 12:1–13 (quoted in part above) David is forced to come face to face with his sin and to take responsibility for his actions.

Reflection or Discussion No. 3

1. What are the acts of violence in the story?
2. What is Jesus' response to the violence directed against him?
3. What does the story suggest to us about how we are to respond to violence?

Crime in the United States

One criminal offense every 2 seconds

One violent crime every 16 seconds

One property crime every 3 seconds

One robbery every 48 seconds

One rape every 5 minutes

One murder every 21 minutes

One larceny theft every 4 seconds

One burglary every 11 seconds

One motor vehicle theft every 20 seconds[4]

We learn that violence against our neighbor is a sin against God. "I have sinned against the LORD," laments David. Violent acts have consequences. David repents of his sins and is forgiven: "The LORD has put away your sin; you shall not die." But the consequences are inescapable: "The sword shall never depart from your house, for you have despised me, and have taken the wife of Uriah the Hittite to be your wife."

The other scripture passage that helps us understand the role of God's people in a violent world is found in Luke 23:13–35. It is the story in which the human community commits violence against the Holy God of heaven in the person of Jesus, nailing him to the cross to die a violent death. Read the story and use the questions (Reflection or Discussion No. 3).

Forgiveness

God desires forgiveness and reconciliation in the place of violence. We as God's people follow that lead and offer restoration of individuals and of the community.

But forgiveness is a tricky thing. What does it mean to offer forgiveness to violent offenders? Does it mean that we find excuses for reprehensible acts, blaming them on all sorts of social ills? Does it mean that we turn our backs on crime and on the victims of crime? Too often well-meaning Christians have been guilty of misunderstanding the nature of forgiveness.

United Church of Christ minister Dr. Marie Fortune, from her years of experience with victims of domestic violence, warns that church people are often too quick to forgive. Meeting with a group of incest offenders in a court-mandated treatment program, she discovered some things about forgiveness. "They made this request of me: Whenever you talk with church people, tell them not to forgive us so quickly."

This group of offenders consisted of church-going men. After their arrests for molesting their own children, each of them had gone directly to his pastor for help. "Each had been prayed over and sent home 'forgiven.' They said it was the worst thing anyone could have done to them, because it allowed them to continue to avoid responsibility for the harm they had done."[5]

Does this mean that we are not to be forgiving people? Not at all, but perhaps we need a new understanding of what forgiveness means. Understanding the nature of forgiveness has always been crucial to an understanding of the Christian faith.

Marjorie J. Thompson offers some help in putting together a complex theological puzzle. She suggests that Christians may often confuse forgiveness with some other things. First of all, Thompson says, forgiving does not mean that we are to deny our hurt. "Forgiveness is a possibility only when we acknowledge the negative impact of someone's actions or attitudes on our lives."

Again, forgiveness must not be an excuse to justify destructive behavior. "To excuse such behaviors—at least in the sense of pretending not to notice or of saying 'Oh, that's all right'—is to tolerate and condone them. Evil actions are not 'all right.' They are sins."

Finally, forgiving is not the same thing as forgetting. Certain behaviors must never be forgotten.

Forgiveness is a choice we can make. It is not, however a choice without cost. [It] "reflects . . . both the manner in which God forgives us and the costliness of that infinite gift. Forgiveness is a decision to call forth and rebuild that love which is the only authentic ground of any human relationship. . . . Indeed, it is only because God continually calls forth and rebuilds this love with us that we are capable of doing so with one another. To forgive is to participate in the mystery of God's love."[6]

Forgiveness: A Biblical Perspective

An individual who sins unintentionally shall present a female goat a year old for a sin offering. And the priest shall make atonement before the LORD for the one who commits an error, when it is unintentional, to make atonement for the person, who then shall be forgiven. For both the native among the Israelites and the alien residing among them—you shall have the same law for anyone who acts in error. But whoever acts high-handedly, whether a native or an alien, affronts the LORD, and shall be cut off from among the people. Because of having despised the word of the LORD and broken his commandment such a person shall be utterly cut off and bear the guilt. (Num. 15:27–31)

Be on your guard! If another disciple sins, you must rebuke the offender, and if there is repentance, you must forgive. And if the same person sins against you seven times a day, and turns back to you seven times and says, "I repent," you must forgive. (Luke 17:3–4)

Christians and Nonviolence

There is a tradition of nonviolence acknowledged by a number of Christian denominations over the centuries. This theology has had one of its most eloquent spokespersons in our own century in the voice of Dr. Martin Luther King Jr. In his first speech to the massed thousands of protesters in Montgomery, Alabama, days after the arrest of Rosa Parks on a city bus, Dr. King said:

Reflection or Discussion No. 4

1. What role do you think forgiveness plays in a Christian response to violence?
2. Think of a situation in which you had difficulty forgiving. *(If you are doing this exercise with a group, you may choose to tell about your experience.)*
3. Think about a time when you were forgiven for a wrong you committed. What was the feeling? *(Again, if you are meeting with a group, you may tell about the experience if you choose to do so.)*

Chapter One: *Violence: A Christian Response* 17

Love must be our regulating ideal. Once again we must hear the words of Jesus echoing across the centuries: "Love your enemies, bless them that curse you, and pray for them that despitefully use you." If we fail to do this, our protest will end up as a meaningless drama on the stage of history, and its memory will be shrouded with the ugly garments of shame. In spite of the mistreatment that we have confronted, we must not become bitter and end up hating our white brothers. As Booker T. Washington said, "Let no man pull you so low as to make you hate him."[7]

This theology of nonviolence has been a hallmark of the faiths of Quakers, Amish, and Mennonites, among other Christian groups. The Mennonites believe that the Sermon on the Mount, which they hold as their creed, prohibits Christians from fighting in battles or holding offices that require them to use force.

Quakers, under the leadership of William Penn, settled Pennsylvania as a haven for those who faced persecution elsewhere. The colony, while under Quaker government, maintained no militia and only a small police force. Quakers are still leaders in the fields of peace education and conflict resolution.

Christian denominations that ascribe to the principle of living nonviolent lives are a small but influential group. It is sometimes helpful for other Christians to study their traditions.

CLOSING

1. Recall a time in your childhood when you felt safe and secure. What gave you the sense of security? If you are doing this study with a group, you may want to tell others about this experience. If you are reading this alone, you may want to write about it in your journal. Put the emphasis on the feelings that you had.
2. Read aloud Psalm 18:1–6.
3. Pray the following prayer:
   O God, we confess that we are by nature a violent people. But you have shown us a different way. Help us to follow in your footsteps. Help us to love one another. Amen.

Chapter Two

Power Structures and Justice

*And what does the L*ORD *require of you
    but to do justice, and to love kindness,
    and to walk humbly with your God?*
                                    Micah 6:8

"It's not fair!"
                        author's 10-year-old son

A WORD AT THE START

As children we all seem to be born with an innate sense of justice. We recognize injustice immediately—especially when we think we are the victims. We are not so sure how to be doers of justice. Micah's counsel is troublesome. "Life is unfair," we find ourselves telling our children.

Life, as we know it, *is* unfair, in our time and in Micah's. African-American mothers are far more likely to give birth to low birth weight infants than are other women in our society. Native Americans were driven off their ancestral lands to live on crowded reservations with infertile soil. Many inner city schools are poorly equipped and in worse condition than their suburban counterparts. Life is unfair.

We are discovering today how economic injustice and racism are often root causes of societal violence. How may Christians address the issues of systemic violence? One inner city gang member who participated in the National Urban Peace and Justice Summit ("the Gang Summit") in Kansas City in 1993 said, "I have to go to school without books. That's violence. I watch TV programs which degrade my people. That's violence. I never see anyone in power who looks like me. That's violence."[1]

Statements like this one force us to rethink our definitions of violence. Perhaps our understanding is too small for the scope of the problem.

Outline for a One-hour Study Session

Prepare for the Session
- Read Chapter 2.
- Gather large sheets of newsprint and markers.

Begin the Session
- Introduce Session 2.
- Read aloud "A Word at the Start."
- Introduce "Activity: Create a Violent Society." Separate the participants into small groups for creating societies. Have the small groups share what they have produced. Lead a discussion using the questions.

Develop the Session
- Ask a volunteer to read aloud "The Violence Iceberg." Point out the diagram of the iceberg.
- Have volunteers read aloud "Joyce's Story" and "Michael's Story." Lead a discussion using "Reflection or Discussion No. 1."
- Lead "Activity" No. 1.
- Read "What About Guns," and use "Reflection or Discussion No. 3."
- Read "Bonds of Injustice: God's Word," and respond to "Reflection and Discussion No. 5."

Conclude the Session
Read in unison the "Closing Prayer."

Activity: Create a Violent Society

Most of us wish that we lived in a more just and nonviolent society. Perhaps one way we can understand why violence is so prevalent is to ask ourselves what we would do if we wanted to create a *violent* society. If possible, work with two or three other people to complete this activity. (Leaders, provide each small group with a large sheet of newsprint and some colored markers.)

Begin by asking yourselves the following question: If you wanted to create the most violent society possible, how would you do it?

Use the following guide to help you to answer the question:
In the society you are creating

- What type of government is there?
- What laws are there?
- What are the punishments for breaking laws?
- What is the educational system?
- What is the family structure (or child-rearing system)?
- What is the role of the media (movies, journalism, TV, etc.)?

You may choose to depict your society in words or pictures. You need not address all of the questions above. In fact, you probably will not be able to. Select the ones that generate responses from the members of your group. If you are doing this study with a large group of people, have each small group describe its imaginary society to the others. Then together discuss the following questions:
1. Which characteristics of these imaginary societies exist in your own country or elsewhere in the world?
2. What would you change about your imaginary society that would make it less violent?
3. What needs to be changed about our real society in order for it to become less violent?

(If you are doing this study on your own, write about your imaginary violent society in your journal.)

The Violence Iceberg

It is helpful to think of violence as an iceberg, with the tip of the iceberg, the only part we can see, being the individual acts of violence against people and property. This is the type of violence that is easy to recognize and to identify as crime. It consists of murder, rape, gang fighting, drive-by shooting, domestic abuse, assault, and terrorism. We can call it *criminal violence.*

But underneath the water lies the other 90 percent of the iceberg of violence, far more threatening and dangerous than the visible tip. Directly below the surface lurks the *institutional violence,* the conditions of our institutions that discriminate against some people, particularly the poor, the elderly, women, children, and people of color. In this category are the schools in the poor neighborhoods that are lacking books, computers, and desks. There are the banks that refuse to grant loans in certain inner-city communities. There are the businesses that don't want to hire people with foreign accents or dark skin or wheelchairs.

Underlying even this kind of institutional violence is the huge unseen base of the iceberg: the violence that is part of our cultural attitudes and "normal" everyday practices. This *cultural violence* includes general attitudes of racism, sexism, ethnocentrism, and homophobia. It is rooted in the me-first attitude that does not recognize the good of the whole community or the rights of other individuals. It includes a general acceptance of violence as an appropriate solution to problems. This kind of violence may be difficult to recognize. It is so pervasive that we have come to accept it as just "the way things are."

The criminal acts that we generally identify as violence may be regarded by the perpetrator as simply a last ditch attempt to regain some control in an oppressive environment. This picture of violence does not excuse cruel and harmful acts. But it does inform us that no solution to the problem that does not look to the base of the iceberg will ever make more than a temporary difference.

"When you violate another person, you're not violating something that has no feeling. You are violating God! And the violation is not just with a gun, or with something you put in folks' bodies. The violation can be done through a law in congress."[2]

The Violence Iceberg

Criminal violence:
• murder, rape, assault, destruction of property

Institutional violence:
• inequality in education and business opportunities
• lack of employment opportunities based on race or gender

Cultural violence:
• Cultural attitudes of racism, sexism, homophobia
• make-my-day mentality
• easy acceptance of violence as normal and acceptable

Joyce's Story

Joyce Tinker lives with three of her children in a tiny, bare motel room in a bleak section of Newark, New Jersey. The room is cold on an icy March afternoon because the motel's heating system has broken down again. Two small boys huddle under the only blanket on the bed watching television. The baby, Keisha, lies in a crib hooked up to a tiny breathing tube connected to an oxygen tank.

Joyce and her children have lived in this motel room for several months, ever since Joyce was raped and beaten in front of her four children in another cheap motel on another side of town. After the rape, the unknown assailant went after Joyce's two boys with a knife, leaving them with ugly scars and uglier nightmares to remind them of the experience.

Earlier on the day of the assault Joyce had called the local police to report harassment by a strange man in the motel parking lot. The police said they could do nothing and never came by to investigate.

Six weeks after the rape, Joyce discovered she was pregnant. That was when she moved, sending her two older children to live with relatives until she could find a more permanent living situation. Joyce planned to put the new baby up for adoption.

She gave birth three months early to little Keisha, who weighed only two and one-half pounds. The tiny infant fought for breath in the neonatal intensive care unit while Joyce spent as much time as possible by her side. Her lungs were not fully developed. She could not eat on her own. For three months, hooked up to a respirator and feeding tubes, she fought off constant infections. Most of the time the hospital staff thought she would die. By the end of three months Keisha had been named the Miracle Baby by the nurses, and Joyce felt that she could not give her up. She had gone through so much already.

To compound the problem, the recent Child Exclusion Act of New Jersey ordained that Joyce could not get the extra $102 each month that she formerly would have received for a new baby. Like other states, New Jersey is attempting to cut down on illegitimate births by withholding financial support.

Joyce lives in her motel room with its paper-thin walls and broken heating system on Aid to Families with Dependent Children and food stamps. Some of the baby's prescription drugs and medical equipment are covered by Medicaid; others are not.

Joyce hopes to find a place to live where her two older daughters can join her. She has given up for a time the idea of looking for a job. Who would take care of the baby with all of her special needs? Besides jobs are difficult to find. Joyce dropped out of high school at the age of sixteen when she became pregnant for the first time.

Reflection or Discussion No. 1

1. What acts of violence do you identify in the stories of Joyce and Michael?
2. Can you identify examples in the stories of:
   (a) criminal violence,
   (b) institutional violence,
   (c) cultural violence?

Reflection or Discussion No. 2

1. What do you see as root causes of violence in your community?
2. Which of the causes identified in "Causes of Violence" do you find most significant in producing violence in a society?

Michael's Story

Linda moved from the inner city to a small apartment in the suburbs when Michael began school. Michael's older brother and sister had both encountered trouble with drugs and street gangs and now as teenagers had both dropped out of school. Robert, seventeen, had spent time in jail for a number of petty crimes.

Michael was bright, and Linda hoped for a better education and a better school environment for him. Paying rent in the suburbs was a stretch for Linda. She worked overtime at her job whenever she could and spent evenings and weekends cleaning people's homes.

Michael did well in school but seldom seemed to play with other children after school. He was the only African-American child in his class and never felt that he fit in. He seemed content to spend time in the small apartment watching TV and playing Nintendo. Linda was just as glad that he stayed home because she was gone so much, and she didn't want to worry about him being out on the streets. Once Michael admitted that the other children made fun of him and didn't want him around.

Neil was the older boy in the neighborhood who made the most trouble for Michael. He teased him and often started fights. Michael once got into trouble for fighting in school when Neil tripped him on the steps on his way to class.

When Michael entered seventh grade, his grades began to drop and he looked for excuses to stay home from school. His mother left for work early in the morning, and often Michael just didn't bother to get out of bed.

When Linda called the school to check on Michael's poor grades, she was shocked at how much school he had missed. The principal claimed that there was nothing he could do to help Michael if he didn't come to school.

One day Linda received a call at work from the school principal. Michael had brought a knife to school and had stabbed Neil. Neil was at the hospital getting stitches in his arm. Michael was at the police station.

Causes of Violence

An ecumenical network in the United States, The Things That Make for Peace: The Churches' Anti-Violence Action Network, has identified some root causes of violence:

1. The violence of unemployment and lack of economic opportunity.
   This situation creates the condition of poverty and lays the groundwork for the violence of poverty, hunger, disease, poor diet, family breakdown, and intense personal stress.

2. The violence of stress.
   Stress produces tension that is often manifested in acts of violence and conflict in the home and neighborhood. This stress over survival leads to a breakdown in relationships in the home and the neighborhood.
3. The violence of low self-esteem.
   This is the violence of internalized oppression of racism and sexism. It manifests itself in acts of violence against others, in black-on-black (self-against-self) crime, and in violence against women. The insidious nature of this violence is manifest in the effort always to blame the victims for the violence they face.
4. The violence between men and women.
   Domestic violence is brought on by the general attitude of sexism that pervades the culture. . . . This violence is manifested in the home and in the day-to-day relationships between men and women. The issue of the use of women as sexual objects . . . is a core dimension of this violence.
5. The violence of the police force and the courts.
   These systems commit acts of violence against urban youth, especially young black men . . . through police harassment, racial insensitivity, and provocative acts that lead to confrontation, resisting arrest, and, often, severe injury and death. In addition to police harassment, the court system condemns these young people . . . to lives without a future. . . . many young people find themselves tried and convicted because of who they are and not what they have done. They . . . find themselves guilty until they prove themselves innocent.
6. The violence of ignorance.
   Ignorance destroys a community's future by depriving it of skills for employment and economic development, an accurate history that promotes self-esteem, . . . and the desire to learn . . . with the excitement of expanding the mind in poetry, art, writing, science, and math.[3]

What About Guns?

Concerns over escalating violence in our society have fueled another type of battle. What is the place of gun ownership by individuals in a free nation? This issue has generated a tremendous amount of anger and political activism on both sides of the question.

The second amendment of the United States Constitution provides that, "A well regulated militia, being necessary to the security of a free State, the right of the people to keep and bear arms shall not be infringed." This amendment has long been a symbol of the freedom of the individual that the United States has always guaranteed. Many people, including the members of the National Rifle Association, have seen any regulation of gun ownership as an infringement of that right.

ACTIVITIES

1. Draw a large version of the Violence Iceberg on newsprint. Invite participants to give examples of situations that belong in each of the three parts of the iceberg. Write these examples on the iceberg.
2. Write a Litany of Confession in which you confess your own involvement in institutional or cultural situations that promote injustice and violence. Use the litany as the closing prayer for the session.

Reflection or Discussion No. 3

1. Can guns be regulated without infringing on the individual's right to be armed?
2. What are dangers to a society of placing limits on the right to bear arms?
3. What are dangers we face if we do not control the trafficking in firearms?
4. What suggestions do you have for limiting the misuse of firearms?

Reflection or Discussion No. 4

1. How would possessions be redistributed in our society today if we were to celebrate a year of jubilee?
2. How would our relationships be different if we celebrated a jubilee?
3. What can people of faith do today as a reminder that resources belong to God?

On the other hand, today as never before, staggering statistics have shown the dangers of the widespread gun ownership that exists in the United States.[4]

- A gun takes the life of a child every two hours—the equivalent of a classroom full every two days.
- Homicide is now the third leading cause of death for elementary and middle school children (ages five to fourteen).
- Between 1979 and 1991, nearly 50,000 children were killed by firearms—a total equivalent to the number of U.S. casualties in the Vietnam War.
- A gun in the home increases the likelihood of homicide threefold. A gun in the home is forty-three times more likely to be used to commit homicide, suicide, or an accidental killing than it is to be used for self-defense.
- Guns are seven times more deadly than all other weapons combined.

Guns are becoming increasingly deadly, available, cheap, and numerous. Proposed legislation for gun control seeks to impose some control over a situation that is out of control.

Opponents of gun regulation point out that illegal trafficking in guns is already so rampant that there is more than a grain of truth in the old slogan, "If guns are outlawed, only outlaws will have guns."

Interestingly, there is no clause in the Canadian Charter of Rights and Freedoms that parallels the second amendment of the United States Constitution. Many Canadians blame the easy accessibility of illegal weapons over the border for the recent increase in violent crime in their nation.

Jubilee

And you shall hallow the fiftieth year and you shall proclaim liberty throughout the land to all its inhabitants. It shall be a jubilee for you: you shall return, every one of you, to your property and every one of you to your family. . . . you shall not cheat one another. (Lev. 25:10, 14b)

The people of ancient Israel had a law that provided for the restoration of justice among a people who tended to go astray. The requirements for the year of jubilee are described in Leviticus 25:8–18. Although there is little evidence that the Israelite people fulfilled all the requirements for the jubilee, the law stood as a reminder that the resources of the nation belonged ultimately to God and not to greedy individuals.

What Is the Role of Law Enforcement?

Is a tough new law enforcement system the cause for the dramatic drop in violent crime in the City of New York? Former Police Commissioner William J. Bratton believes that it is. Discrediting traditional explanations for crime such as poverty or the breakdown of family or community, Commissioner Bratton proposed fighting crime with a tough crack-down on criminals.

Kansas City saw a sharp decline in crime recently when police began confiscating illegal guns and strictly enforcing existing laws.

Violent crime is on the decline in many U.S. cities. There are several possible reasons for this blip in the screen. Demographics account for part of it. The group responsible for the most crime— 15- to 29-year-old males—is simply smaller than when the baby-boomer generation set off the crime wave in the 1960s.

Stricter sentencing laws have assured that repeat, violent offenders (those responsible for a disproportionate amount of crime) are in jails and off the streets.

Some places have seen a decline in the use of crack, which was associated with so much crime in the 1980s.

But many criminologists maintain that a new kind of policing has something to do with the drop in crime.

One block in New Orleans was labeled "the most dangerous block in the U.S." because of the drug dealing, turf battles, and drive-by shootings that turned it into an inner-city war zone. Three killings each month were the norm for the street. But things are different now. Police have set up substations in vacant buildings staffed by officers on foot patrol. The police are getting to know the citizens and have begun spending time with the children and teen-agers. Killing has gone down 74 percent.

Many towns are sending their police officers back to the streets. Walking the beat instead of cruising by in a police car puts the officers back in touch with the community. Precinct offices offer recreational, tutoring, and scholarship programs for young people. The personal contact between police and people is helping to restore trust. Policing style has shifted from racking up arrests to problem solving.[5]

Media attention has shown how often police have been the initiators of violence in several high-profile criminal cases in the United States and Canada. Racism and violence have been common accusations against police forces.

However, one message that is clear is that any attempt at reducing crime must include the law enforcement officials in the solution.

Reflection or Discussion No. 5

1. What is the message of these scripture passages concerning justice?
2. According to the scriptures, what are the consequences of living unjust lives?
3. What are the consequences of promoting justice?
4. What can we learn about the role of faithful people in today's world?

Bonds of Injustice: God's Word

For from the least to the greatest of them,
> everyone is greedy for unjust gain;
and from prophet to priest,
> everyone deals falsely.
They have treated the wound of my people carelessly,
> saying, "Peace, peace,"
> when there is no peace.
They acted shamefully, they committed abomination;
> yet they were not ashamed,
> they did not know how to blush.
Therefore they shall fall among those who fall;
> at the time that I punish them, they shall be overthrown,
says the LORD. (Jer. 6:13–15)

Woe to him who builds his house by unrighteousness,
> and his upper rooms by injustice;
who makes his neighbors work for nothing,
> and does not give them their wages, . . .
Did not your father eat and drink and do justice and righteousness?
> Then it was well with him.
He judged the cause of the poor and needy;
> then it was well.
Is not this to know me?
> says the LORD,
But your eyes and heart
> are only on your dishonest gain,
for shedding innocent blood,
> and for practicing oppression and violence. (Jer. 22:13, 15–17)

Is not this the fast that I choose:
> to loose the bonds of injustice,
> to undo the thongs of the yoke,
to let the oppressed go free,
> and to break every yoke?
Is it not to share your bread with the hungry,
> and bring the homeless poor into your house;
when you see the naked, to cover them,
> and not to hide yourself from your own kin? . . .

If you offer your food to the hungry
>   and satisfy the needs of the afflicted, . . .
The LORD will guide you continually,
>   and satisfy your needs in parched places,
>   and make your bones strong;
and you shall be like a watered garden,
>   like a spring of water, . . .
you shall be called the repairer of the breach,
>   the restorer of streets to live in. (Isa. 58:6–7, 10–12)

When he came to Nazareth, where he had been brought up, he went to the synagogue on the sabbath day, as was his custom. He stood up to read, and the scroll of the prophet Isaiah was given to him. He unrolled the scroll and found the place where it was written:
"The Spirit of the Lord is upon me,
because he has anointed me
>   to bring good news to the poor.
He has sent me to proclaim release to the captives
>   and recovery of sight to the blind,
>   to let the oppressed go free,
to proclaim the year of the Lord's favor." (Luke 4:16–19)

CLOSING PRAYER

Forgive us, O God, for eating too much when there are hungry children in our cities.

Forgive us for complaining that we don't have the right clothes to wear when our neighbor has no winter coat.

Forgive us for using up so many of the world's resources when there are many people who have never lived in a home with central heating or indoor plumbing.

Forgive us for taking all that we have for granted.

Teach us, O God, to have grateful hearts and generous spirits.

In the name of the One who broke the bread and shared it with all. Amen.

Chapter Three
Violence, Children, and Youth

"Let the little children come to me."
Mark 10:14

A WORD AT THE START

Evidence has shown that some violent crimes such as burglary and even murder may actually be on the decrease in recent years. This is encouraging news. However, there is one area in which the statistics are not encouraging. Our children and youth are dramatically more involved in crime than ever before, both as victims and as perpetrators. That is news that scares even the most hardened of us. We all have stereotypical images in our minds of the violent criminal. The ten-year-old child carrying a semiautomatic weapon to school in his book bag does not fit any of them.

The wave of youth violence is so frightening because it seems arbitrary, out of control, and unfathomable. As Christians we have been called to "welcome the child." How do we show God's love to the child who has become unlovable? Are we willing to waste an entire generation of urban youth who have exchanged their school books and baseball gloves for drugs and deadly weapons? Are there any throw-away children in the family of God?

Children have always been vulnerable as victims of violence because they are small, weak, and dependent. In our culture, however, the children and youth have also become a frightening source of violence. Many adults live in fear of the children and teenagers and their families in their neighborhoods. Christians are called to follow Jesus' example of welcoming and defending the children.

Outline for a One-hour Study Session

Prepare for the Session
- Read Chapter 3.
- Collect recent newspapers, news magazines, scissors.
- Make arrangements and gather materials for creating a bulletin board, poster, or album.

Begin the Session
- Read aloud "What Is the Problem?" having participants take turns reading the statements marked by bullets. (Allow those who choose not to read aloud to say "pass" when it is their turn.)
- Create a bulletin board, poster, or album using the "Activity."
- Read "Juvenile Justice?" and "Some Alternatives."
- Ask a volunteer to read aloud "What Can the Churches Do?" and "Churches Getting Involved," and lead a discussion using "Reflection or Discussion No. 1."
- Lead "Activity No. 3."

Conclude the Session
- Use the "Bible Study" and "Reflection or Discussion No. 2" on page 43, or read aloud Mark 10:13–14.
- Pray in unison the "Closing Prayer."

What Is the Problem?

We open our morning newspapers and find stories that we cannot begin to understand, stories such as these.

- Louis was a student in a prestigious suburban school district. For years he had been harassed at the bus stop by a group of bullies that teased and taunted him, stole his hat and his homework papers, poked, pushed, and punched him. Although the situation had been reported numerous times to school authorities and the offenders each time had been detained after school, the situation never really changed. Finally, when Louis was in ninth grade, one day he took a gun to school in his backpack. When one of the offenders began the usual taunting, Louis pulled out the gun and shot him dead.
- Sharon was a cheerleader and homecoming queen candidate at her high school. When it became clear that another student was likely to be elected cheerleading captain and homecoming queen, Sharon's mother allegedly tried to hire a hit man to kill the other girl.
- Rainey made drug deliveries for a dealer in Chicago. In return, he was rewarded with gifts like expensive sneakers, video games, and a bicycle. Rainey was nine years old. The dealer used him and other young messengers because they were less likely to be suspected by police. Rainey was mouthy and aggressive. One day an angry customer, annoyed by his taunting, shot and killed him.
- A group of children standing at a school bus stop one morning was mowed down by a volley of fire from a semiautomatic handgun in a drive-by shooting gone awry. The school crossing guard threw herself in front of the children to protect them from the blast and was killed instantly. Two children died from bullet wounds. Several others were hospitalized.
- Joan was a graduate student at McMaster University in Hamilton, Ontario. She was studying in her apartment after dinner. A former boyfriend entered her apartment and shot her in the back, abdomen, arms, and legs. She was lying dead in a pool of blood when her roommate returned to the apartment.

The problem of youth violence is not limited to North America. Violence by and against young people presents a horrifying picture all over the world:

- In Colombia death squads exterminated dozens of children from the *pandillas* (gangs) in a campaign against "street vermin" and "social undesirables."

- The United Nations Commission on Human Rights confirmed torture of children in nineteen countries and child executions in twenty-two.
- The worldwide failure to meet the needs of the world's 100 million street children amounts to what Anglican Bishop Luiz Osorio Prado of Brazil calls "a form of ethnic cleansing."
- Children in Guatemala have had ears or tongues cut off or eyes gouged by police.
- The abandoned street children in Guatemala City often gather together in groups for safety. The groups seem to mimic a family structure. The society calls these groups "gangs."
- In Canada the Young Offenders Act adopted in 1984 to address youth crime assures that some youth face harsher penalties than adults committing the same offenses.
- In schools in Canada and the United States, children involved in violent incidents are expelled from school despite the fact that often there are no alternative educational programs available for them. This situation tends to lead to more violence, not less.
- Over 18,000 children in the United States are abused or neglected each day.
- An average U.S. child will have witnessed 18,000 murders on television by the time she or he is eighteen years old.
- Canadian youth are dropping out of school and running away from home in record numbers or being driven from home by abusive parents. In Quebec, 36 percent of students will never finish high school. The dropout rate is closer to 60 percent in some low-income districts. Vancouver, Toronto, and Montreal are centers for runaways, gangs, prostitutes, and drug addicts. Eight thousand people under the age of thirty live on the streets of Montreal; in Toronto there may be 10,000 homeless people under the age of twenty-four.
- Half of the Canadians who use the food banks are young people.
- All over the world, young people who have little hope for collective improvement in their situation turn instead to individual survival. The means to survival may include violent crime, drug dealing, robbery, begging, and prostitution. Gang affiliation and gang warfare are the results.
- One million U.S. teenagers are victims of violent crimes each year.
- "The killing of our street children is like a national spiritual suicide," warns Bishop Osorio. "Our response must be something more than nausea, indignation or fright."[1]

ACTIVITY

Look through newspapers and newsmagazines for stories of children who have been victims or perpetrators of violent crimes. Make a bulletin board, poster, or album to display these articles and pictures.

- In the United States, homicide is the third leading cause of death for children aged five to fourteen, the second leading cause for those between fifteen and twenty-four.
- More that 10,000 young people in the United States between the ages ten and twenty-four are murdered or commit suicide annually.
- While juveniles account for 10 percent of the U.S. population, they are 25 percent of the victims of violent crime.
- Over 3 million crimes occur in U.S. public schools each year, including thirty-five deaths and ninety-two injuries caused by guns.
- Eleven percent of teachers and 23 percent of students report having been the victim of an act of violence in school. Thirteen percent of the students and 2 percent of the teachers say they have carried a weapon to school.[2]

Juvenile Justice?

Canada and the United States have the highest incarceration rates for youth in the industrialized world. What is the role of the juvenile justice system in the midst of this bleak picture of youth violence? The system for years has been so overloaded that many young offenders receive little attention from the system until they have become "hardened criminals." The punishments that are meted out often do more to confirm the young person in a life of crime than to provide any substantial rehabilitation. There is a tendency in the United States and Canada toward increasingly harsh sentences for young offenders. The government in Ontario announced its "zero tolerance" on violence in schools, recommending swift expulsion for those involved in acts of violence.

The new crime bill in the United States calls for a half billion dollars to be spent on new prisons for "violent and chronic" juvenile offenders. Already 500,000 juveniles are locked in adult jails.

Alternative methods of sentencing are proposed but often are far more expensive than the traditional incarceration. Boot camps that involve strict discipline, military-style drills, classes, counseling sessions, close supervision, mentoring, and trust-building cost much more than prison (in Pennsylvania, at least twice as much). Do they make a difference? It is too soon to tell whether the lower recidivism rates are because of the program's merits or because of the carefully chosen participants.

Community-based rehabilitation programs that address issues of addiction, job training, and literacy seem to be effective but often receive inadequate community and financial support.

What happens when rehabilitated teenagers return to dysfunctional homes and violent neighborhoods? When the conditions at home have not changed, it is easy for past offenders to return to a familiar life of crime.

Programs offered by schools, communities, churches, mosques, and temples that attempt to work with at-risk youngsters before they have a chance to become criminal offenders seem to be the most helpful. Educational and recreational opportunities, spiritual growth experiences, job and skill training, counseling, and mentoring by positive role models make a difference in many cases.

Some Alternatives

A coalition of four United Methodist churches in the Philadelphia area offers a program called Youth Corps as an alternative to incarceration. These youth in crisis are poor, are mostly from single-parent families, are failing in school, and have a history of drug abuse.

The program of mentoring, skill training, and business opportunities offers an alternative to incarceration. The young people are able to sleep at home but attend programming offered by Youth Corps during the day and early evening hours.

Participants operate a furniture-refinishing business and a card printing shop through which they learn trades as well as business skills such as marketing, finance, and a work ethic. Meanwhile they maintain connections with the positive role models who staff the program.

❖

The means to acceptance and self-esteem for young people growing up in certain sections of Los Angeles have too often been linked to drugs, gangs, and crime. A few young people with a commitment to their Christian faith wanted to present an alternative.

The United Methodist Junior Basketball League (UMJBL) began in 1988 when two teenagers started a local church basketball team and initiated games with several neighboring churches. The program has the goals of enhancing youth self-esteem, developing social responsibility, and providing role models who demonstrate Christian values.

Since its inception, the UMJBL has grown in size and gained an ecumenical base of support. It provides job training, counseling, and job-referral services as well as athletic opportunities, while at the same time remaining grounded in Christian witness, mission, and evangelism.

❖

When south-central Los Angeles was torn apart by rioting in 1992, its neighbors in Fresno, California, realized that their city with its high percentage of urban poor, racial-ethnic groups, and recent immigrants was similarly vulnerable. Christians of many denominations, ethnicities, and socioeconomic backgrounds came together to pray for their city. Meeting monthly in the top floors of city buildings, they looked out over the city and prayed for its people. They tried to discover the needs of the community.

During one meeting at Juvenile Hall, where young offenders are incarcerated, the group received a challenge to get involved with troubled youth. As a result, over 3,000 Christian volunteers began working in the juvenile justice system and with at-risk young people.

❖

The National Council of the Churches of Christ in the U.S.A. annually recognizes ecumenical and interreligious organizations that initiate projects that offer creative models. One group to receive recognition in 1994 was the Southern Area Clergy Council (SACC) of Los Angeles for their project KEEP IT GOOD, IN THE HOOD (neighbor*hood*). The program is faith-based and participatory. It addresses violence and empowerment. Included are an entrepreneurial academy, a violence prevention conference for congregations, and a youth athletic league. It is widely promoted in the community with buttons, flyers, and billboards. "We're not waiting for the mayor to make our community better. We're taking it upon ourselves in the churches to make the community better," says SACC director Romie Lilly.[3]

❖

"As casualties of systemic warfare that drives so-called 'undesirables' out of the mainstream, our culture has managed to produce its share of outlaws. Except to lock them up or to snuff them out, we probably know little else about how to deal with them. More importantly, when it comes to making the transition and living inside the law, former outlaws, gangsters and anti-social youngsters know little about how to deal with themselves."[4]

The Break and Build Program of Kansas City came out of the Peace and Justice Summit (a conference on gang-related violence) held in 1993 in that city. It provides help for at-risk young people through education, counseling, and leadership training. Churches and community organizations work together to prepare young people to lead productive lives.

What Can the Churches Do?

In a survey of 126 Protestant young people concerning their experiences of violence, the students were asked to respond in essay form to the question: What should the church do about violence in our communities? Here are some of their responses:

- The church should give children an alternative to gangs by having such programs as after-school sports, drama, field trips, and Bible studies. Violence in the home is another situation that should be dealt with openly in the church.
- The church's greatest influence can be in striving to end violence within families. By being available in counseling and caring capacities, the church can educate children about their rights in the family and offer a "safe house" to discuss their problems.
- The church should provide a program for people who have been abused in any way. Ministers, counselors, and just plain "good listeners" could be recruited to help people work through their problems.
- The church should do something to try and get violence off television. If something is done to stop the younger generations from being exposed to violence, many problems would not occur.[5]

Churches have one important resource in a crowded city. They have space. Often, with problems of falling membership, what they really have is too much space. One thing churches can offer is safe space for children and youth. Many churches open their doors for only a few hours each week. Christians can regain a vision of the church as sanctuary, a holy place, a place where children whose lives are filled with fear and anger and brutality can encounter safety and love, nurturing and beauty. Youth need education, vocational training, mentoring, and positive role models. All of these can be found in churches.

The Reverend Leonard Comithier is assistant commissioner of New York State Division of Youth. He stresses that there has been a "stunning increase" in youth-related violent crimes, pointing out that violence is so common that "modern society seems to come to accept it as normal. It is here that the moral voice of a community must speak."

Has the church reneged on its responsibility of being that "moral voice" in our society?

The church has always been a bastion of volunteerism. That tradition can offer up volunteers for community service. Church members can also join together to lobby for changes in public policy.

Churches Getting Involved

How can churches begin to work on issues of violence?

The first step is to *pray* about the issues. We acknowledge God's leadership in all that we do. We need to turn to God with our needs and our brokenness.

Next, we learn to *listen*. How can we begin to understand the needs of our communities unless we hear from the people who are directly involved? Glide Memorial United Methodist Church in San

Reflection or Discussion No. 1

1. How has your congregation or organization done in each of the following areas:
   - PRAYER
   - LISTENING
   - TELLING THE STORY
   - RESPONSE
2. What are some specific ways that you could improve in each of the four areas?
3. How can your church become a safe place for children?
4. What services does your community provide for children and teenagers in the areas of
   - recreation
   - counseling
   - academic assistance (tutoring, testing, special help for learning disabled, and so forth)
   - career training and counseling
   - scholarship aid
   - psychological services
5. What are some of the areas of need?
6. How might your church or a group of churches fill some of the gaps?

Francisco is a congregation that goes out into the streets on Sunday mornings to invite the community in. Other churches send out parish visitors, not to preach but to listen to the stories of the people in the community.

As people of faith we *tell our faith story*. We are willing to be vulnerable, to share in a personal way how God has been with us in the midst of our own brokenness, how Jesus was willing to die on the cross for our own sins.

We *respond* to the needs of the people around us. Too often church people have felt that they have all the answers. "The people who are the experts, who have the answers, are the people who live in the community," explains the Reverend John Schol, director of the "Shalom Zone" urban ministries program for the United Methodist Board of Global Ministries. People are empowered when they are part of the solution. Congregations have resources available to them that can be of help in the solution, resources such as space, money, community, and willing volunteers, people with education and skills who are willing to share their gifts and their community. Their job is to make these resources available to those who need them.

Children of War

Arn Chorn saw his family murdered by the Khmer Rouge in Cambodia. At the age of fourteen, he was sent to fight against the Vietnamese. He witnessed acts of torture and brutality before arriving as a refugee in the United States at the age of eighteen. Many of the survivors of the Khmer Rouge did not want to talk about their experiences in Cambodia. Chorn found that speaking of the horrors eased his pain.

Out of his experiences came Children of War, an organization that brings together young survivors of international combat zones. The young people come together from El Salvador, Northern Ireland, Haiti, South Africa, as well as from the violence-torn ghettos of the United States. They tell their stories to young people in churches, synagogues, community centers, and schools. At the same time they provide support, understanding, and healing for one another.

Jacob Smith and Donovan McCoy grew up in the Bedford-Stuyvesant section of Brooklyn, well-acquainted with crime, gang violence, racism, and poverty. They joined Children of War after serving time in prison. Both young men credit Children of War with turning their lives around. The organization offered them support and encouragement that they were unable to find elsewhere.

Local branches of Children of War continue to touch lives. They have had a powerful impact and serve as models for other programs ministering to young people.

The Violence of War

Zlata Filipovic began keeping a diary in 1991 as an eleven-year-old girl in Sarajevo. Soon after she began, war closed in on her city, sending many of her friends into exile, destroying her city, and drastically changing her life. Here is an excerpt from her diary.

Monday, 29 June, 1992

BOREDOM!!! SHOOTING!!! SHELLING!!! PEOPLE BEING KILLED!!! DESPAIR!!! HUNGER!!! MISERY!!! FEAR!!!

That's my life! The life of an innocent eleven-year-old schoolgirl!! A schoolgirl without a school, without the fun and excitement of school. A child without games, without friends, without the sun, without birds, without nature, without fruit, without chocolate or sweets, with just a little powdered milk. In short, a child without a childhood. A wartime child. I now realize that I am really living through a war, I am witnessing an ugly, disgusting war. I and thousands of other children in this town that is being destroyed, that is crying, weeping, seeking help, but getting none. God, will this ever stop, will I ever be a schoolgirl again, will I ever enjoy my childhood again? I once heard that childhood is the most wonderful time of your life. And it is. I loved it, and now an ugly war is taking it all away from me. Why? I feel sad. I feel like crying. I am crying.[6]

Wherever there is war, children are the victims. Zlata speaks for millions who are voiceless.

Homeless Youth

A growing segment of the homeless population in North America consists of children and youth, many of whom have no family ties. Many have chosen life on the streets in preference to abusive home situations. They discover, however, that escape from abusive homes does not end the violence of their lives. Homeless youth face harassment from police, other adults in authority, and from citizens who want them out of the streets. Curfew laws and loitering ordinances designed to make the streets safer for citizens often turn homeless youth into criminals.

- Children and youth of our nation are dying on our streets, in roller-skating rinks, in schools, in homes, and on playgrounds.
- Many of our children cannot play in playgrounds or sit on their front porches without a bullet piercing their skulls.
- The escalation of violence on our nation's streets has reached epidemic proportions. Young black men ages 15 to 24 are six times more likely to be killed than other Americans of similar age.
- Almost all of our communities are facing a crack cocaine crisis of epidemic proportions. Every seven minutes a child is arrested for a drug offense.
- Twenty-five percent of young black males between 23 and 29 are in prison. More black males are incarcerated at some stage of the criminal justice system than are enrolled in institutions of higher education.
- Every 53 minutes a child dies because of poverty.
- Every eight seconds an American child drops out of school.

—*Yvonne Delk*

- Many of our young people face daily the lures of drugs, sex, fast money, and guns; these are the unnoticed youth who operate in a maddening universe where things always seem to go wrong.
- Our children and our youth are not being educated, nurtured, matured, or disciplined in their hearts, minds, and bodies.[7]

—*Yvonne Delk*

Shelters for the homeless sometimes do not welcome young people because they have different needs from adults. In shelters youth often become the prey of adult residents.

A large percentage (perhaps as many as 35 percent) of homeless youth identify themselves as gay or lesbian. They endure physical abuse, scorn, and rejection by homophobic peers.

Benjamine Wojcik is an AmeriCorps (U.S. national domestic service organization) member and a formerly homeless person himself. Benjamine is seeking to help homeless young people tell their own stories. He teaches them to use video cameras and to make statements that are shown on cable TV. He encourages the young people to take action to make a difference in their own situations.

What About the Youngest Children?

When we think about problems of violence in the lives of young people, our thoughts most often turn to teenagers, but there is a segment of the young population whose problems are often invisible to the rest of society. They are the ones who cannot speak for themselves. They are the very "least of these."

Physical abuse is the leading cause of death for children under a year old. Ten percent of all deaths of children between one and four years of age are caused by homicide.

- "In 1990, almost 90 percent of those children who died as a result of abuse or neglect were under age 5; 53 percent were under age 1."
- "One third of all sexual abuse cases involve children under six years of age."[8]

The Role of the Schools

Some states are considering legislation to provide schools with more authority to ensure a safe learning environment such as alternative programs for "disruptive students." Other legislation requires school districts to report acts of violence to police and requires extended suspension for students carrying weapons to school.

One school organized a 100-member Violence Prevention Coalition comprised of parents, teachers, school administrators, social service agencies, law enforcement officials, representatives from the community, and government. The group determined that working together they could make a difference. Coming out of the group's work have been a new school safety plan, a district-wide weapons policy, conflict resolution instruction, peer mediation and conflict management programs, student support groups, training for school staff, school-based probation, family counseling opportunities, school-based drug and alcohol rehabilitation programs, and mental health treatment centers.

The program is already beginning to make a difference. The teachers almost immediately began to notice a substantial decrease in the number of fights. The program coordinators credit the comprehensive approach of the efforts against violence.

Another school says that getting parents involved in the antiviolence program has been the key to its success.

Many schools are initiating peer mediation programs to help students work out their differences. Conflict, they learn, is a natural and healthy part of human interaction. There are healthy and unhealthy ways of responding to conflict. Through role-playing and discussion, students learn to listen to one another and work out solutions to their differences. Peer mediators receive intensive training in how to structure mediation sessions and how to listen actively while being objective.

Lowell Elementary School in Fresno, California, was on the verge of being shut down. One of the poorest schools in the city, it was considered unsafe for the children. Its test scores were abominable; teachers were difficult to recruit.

Christian volunteers from a number of churches volunteered to tutor students, supervise the playground, and help out in classrooms, cafeteria, and halls. Reading levels have risen significantly, and the school is no longer on the city's at-risk list.

Part of the Solution

Young people are often feared, avoided, or blamed for the problems in our society. But how often do we look to our young people to take responsibility for providing solutions to society's ills?

It was with exactly that purpose in mind, however, that the Urban Youth Summit of 1995 assembled inner-city teenagers in Washington, D.C., to propose new ways of dealing with urban violence.

The young people developed plans for controlling violence in their cities and neighborhoods and then visited Capitol Hill to present their visions to their senators and representatives.

One conclusion from the discussions: children want to be safe. When they feel unsafe, they feel the need to arm themselves and take the offensive. Children cannot learn or grow unless they feel safe and secure within a community.

A Lament

Children, children, oh my children! What are we giving you for your future? How do we show our love beyond the wrapped presents tucked under the tree, put in stockings, hidden near the candelabra? We pray for your safety and still sell guns. We pray for your health and still fight over health care for all of you. We pray that you will be strong in your faith, and

ACTIVITIES

1. Take a field trip to a large toy store in the community. Count how many of the toys teach violence. Make a list of these toys. You may want to publish your list in your church's newsletter early in the Christmas season with a recommendation to parents that they avoid buying these toys for the celebration of the birthday of the Prince of Peace.

2. Adopt a school. Select a public school in your city or neighborhood. Make a covenant to pray regularly for the teachers, administrators, and students. Provide services that complement the school program such as after-school child care, tutoring, or recreation. Recruit church members to volunteer their time to help out in the classrooms. Talk to the school principal and PTA regularly about ways your church can help.

3. Read the lament on page 41. Explain that a lament is an expression of sorrow or grief. It is a literary form frequently encountered in scripture. See Psalm 22 for a familiar example of a person of faith crying out in despair at a time when God seems far away.

Try writing your own lament for the world's children. Use it as a prayer in your church's worship service or print it in your church newsletter.

still we weaken the religious family with constant bickering over differences. We care about your education, but we cannot agree how to shape it or pay for it. We want you to be good citizens of your city, your country, your world, but we want you to do it without it costing us anything. We say we do not believe in child labor, but we vote for international trade agreements that allow exploitation of young children in factories and sweatshops around the world. We are afraid of death, of violence, of taxes, and yet we want you to grow up bold, brave and generous. Oh my children, my children, what are we giving you for your future.[9]

Bible Study

Hear, O Israel: The LORD is our God, the LORD alone. You shall love the LORD your God with all your heart, and with all your soul, and with all your might. Keep these words that I am commanding you today in your heart. Recite them to your children and talk about them when you are at home and when you are away, when you lie down and when you rise. Bind them as a sign on your hand, fix them as an emblem on your forehead, and write them on the doorposts of your house and on your gates. (Deut. 6:4–9)

At that time the disciples came to Jesus and asked, "Who is the greatest in the kingdom of heaven?" He called a child, whom he put among them, and said, "Truly I tell you, unless you change and become like children, you will never enter the kingdom of heaven. Whoever becomes humble like this child is the greatest in the kingdom of heaven. Whoever welcomes one such child in my name welcomes me.

"If any of you put a stumbling block before one of these little ones who believe in me, it would be better for you if a great millstone were fastened around your neck and you were drowned in the depth of the sea." (Matt. 18:1–6)

Train children in the right way,
    and when old, they will not stray. (Prov. 22:6)

People were bringing little children to him in order that he might touch them; and the disciples spoke sternly to them. But when Jesus saw this, he was indignant and said to them, "Let the little children come to me; do not stop them; for it is to such as these that the kingdom of God belongs." (Mark 10:13–14)

Reflection or Discussion No. 2

1. What is the role of children in God's world?
2. How can we "train children in the right way?"
3. What can we learn from the children in our lives?

CLOSING PRAYER

There are children in our cities, O God, who must sleep on the floor each night to keep them safe from stray bullets. We pray that they might have peaceful dreams. There are children who never know the joy of running barefoot through grassy fields because their worlds are made of broken glass and concrete. We pray that we might help create a new world where they may run and dance. We pray for children who are more familiar with the shriek of a police siren than a mother's lullaby. We pray for those who have never known the protection of a father's lap. We pray to you, Protector God, that you will blanket your children with safety in an insecure world. We pray that we might hear and answer your call to welcome the little ones. Amen.

CHAPTER FOUR
Thorns of Pain and Fear: Domestic Violence

Husbands, love your wives, just as Christ loved the church.
Eph. 5:25a

A WORD AT THE START

It is a large and frightening world out there. We have learned from childhood to beware of strangers, to be strong and tough, not to put up with anything from anybody. The world seems a hostile place, and we are glad to be able to retreat to the safety of our own homes. Or are we? For many, particularly women, children, and the elderly, home is the most dangerous place to be. Domestic violence goes on behind closed doors. It is often accompanied by so much guilt, shame, and emotional abuse that the victim feels she (or he) must be at fault. There is no safe place to run for protection. Victims often endure ignominy for years; many endure it until it kills them.

Domestic abuse is no respecter of economic status, race, or age. It is a hidden crime, one that the church has been guilty of helping to keep silent. Our task as Christians is to become protectors of the "least of these" and to provide help for the offenders.

Assault by a partner is the leading cause of injury to women aged fifteen to forty-four. Perhaps 35 percent of the emergency room visits made by women are for injuries caused by partner abuse, although the exact number is difficult to calculate because so few victims are willing to blame their batterers.

Women who have been beaten by their male partners are more likely to abuse their children than are nonbattered women. Women and men who grow up in homes where battering occurs may view the situation as "normal" and "private" and are less likely to resist or report the beatings as crimes.

Outline for a One-hour Study Session

Prepare for the Session
- Read Chapter 4.
- Prepare copies of the "Violence Grid" (page 63).

Begin the Session
- Introduce the session.
- Read "A Word at the Start."
- Use the activity and discussion questions in "What Does the Scripture Say?"

Develop the Session
- Have volunteers read aloud "Violence Against Women: The Facts" and "A Global Problem."
- Read "Being There for the Victims" and respond to "Reflection or Discussion No. 1."
- Read "Some Practical Advice."
- Separate the participants into three smaller groups to read "Stories of Domestic Violence" and to respond to "Reflection and Discussion No. 2."
- Read aloud "Ideas for Action" and discuss an appropriate plan of action for your congregation or group.

Conclude the Session
- Pray in unison.
- Distribute copies of the "Violence Grid" and ask participants to keep records of their television viewing during the week. They may take extra copies and engage their family in the survey.

What Does Scripture Say?

Husbands, love your wives, just as Christ loved the church and gave himself up for her, in order to make her holy by cleansing her with the washing of water by the word, so as to present the church to himself in splendor, without a spot or wrinkle or anything of the kind—yes, so that she may be holy and without blemish. In the same way, husbands should love their wives as they do their own bodies. He who loves his wife loves himself. For no one ever hates his own body, but he nourishes and tenderly cares for it, just as Christ does for the church, because we are members of his body. "For this reason a man will leave his father and mother and be joined to his wife, and the two will become one flesh." This is a great mystery, and I am applying it to Christ and the church. Each of you, however, should love his wife as himself, and a wife should respect her husband.

Children, obey your parents in the Lord, for this is right. "Honor your father and mother"—this is the first commandment with a promise: "so that it may be well with you and you may live long on the earth."

And, fathers, do not provoke your children to anger, but bring them up in the discipline and instruction of the Lord. (Eph. 5:25–6:4)

If you are using this study with a group, have someone read the above passage aloud slowly as the group listens with eyes closed. Explain that at the end of the reading you will allow a few moments of silence for participants to meditate on the passage. After a brief time of silence, ask the following questions:
1. What feelings came to you as you listened to the reading from Ephesians?
2. Paul expresses his own confusion about whether the passage is directed toward earthly families or toward the "family" of Christ and the church. What meaning do you think it has for relationships in our earthly families?

There are some scripture passages that give very painful pictures of abusive behavior toward women. Read one or more of the following passages aloud: Gen. 34, Gen. 38, Judg. 11:29–40, 2 Sam. 13.

Try to hear each passage from the point of view of the woman involved. Ask the following questions:
1. How do you think the woman was feeling?
2. In what way was she wronged?
3. What (if any) was the punishment for the wrongdoing? Was the punishment appropriate?
4. What kind of reconciliation took place?

46   Chapter Four: Thorns of Pain and Fear: Domestic Violence

Violence Against Women: The Facts

1. The number one health risk to women in the United States is violent attacks by men. According to the Surgeon General's office, domestic violence caused more injuries to women in 1992 than rapes, muggings, and car accidents combined.
2. Compared with other women, those who have been attacked:

   - are twice as likely to miscarry and four times as likely to bear a child with low birth-weight if attacked during pregnancy;
   - are five times as likely to commit suicide;
   - are four times as likely to seek psychiatric treatment;
   - have an increased risk of alcohol abuse, drug dependence, chronic pain, and depression;
   - face increased costs for medical care including emergency rooms, physician visits, and outpatient care. In 1992, the American Medical Association estimated the costs of domestic violence at five to ten billion dollars a year in health-care expenditures, lost wages, criminal litigation and incarceration; five billion in foster care, and three to five billion in lost services to employers.
   - have two-and-a-half times the health costs of women who aren't battered;
   - have increased risk of pregnancy and of HIV and other sexually transmitted diseases. Since 1990 there has been a dramatic rise in the number of battered women and children who are HIV positive.

3. A woman is ten times more likely to be raped than to die in a car crash.
4. Every eighteen seconds, a woman is beaten. Three to four million women are battered each year.
5. As many as one-third of all women will be physically assaulted by a partner or ex-partner during their lifetimes.
6. Every hour, sixteen women confront rapists; a woman is raped every six minutes.
7. According to one recent study, 29 percent of all forcible rapes occur when the victim is less than eleven years old, while another 32 percent occur between the ages of eleven and seventeen.
8. The crime rate against women in the United States is significantly higher than in other countries. The United States has a rape rate thirteen times higher than England, nearly four times higher than Germany, and more than twenty times higher than Japan.
9. Domestic violence is the single most significant source of injuries to women in the United States.
10. Each year, nearly two million married women and an additional several million single and separated women are battered by intimate partners.

"Of all the health and human service challenges we face, perhaps the most devastating and, ironically, the most preventable is the epidemic of violence sweeping across this nation. Violence is not some mysterious bacterial infection or inexplicable new disease; rather, it is a phenomenon for which we are responsible, and we can prevent it. It is time we stopped the denial and claimed our power to halt the bloodshed and save lives."[1]

—*Donna E. Shalala*

What Is This Violence?

It is physical violence: punching, kicking, slapping, throwing objects, using weapons (knives, bats, cars, acid).

It is sexual violence: forced sexual activity, often following a beating.

It is psychological violence: not unlike brainwashing, similar to what hostages experience.

It is psychological coercion backed by the threat of violence.

It is the destruction of property and pets—always the object or pet that belongs to the victim so the message is clear, "This time it is the dog; next time it is you."

I use the term *violence* conservatively. By violence I mean the use of physical force or the threat of physical force to control another person.[3]

—*Marie M. Fortune*

---

11. Thirty to 35 percent of women who visit emergency rooms seek treatment for injuries related to domestic violence.

12. Ninety-two percent of battered women do not discuss the abuse with their physicians.[2]

A Global Problem

Violence against women is a problem throughout the world. Girl children and adolescents are unwanted and abused in many countries. In Peru, 90 percent of the young mothers aged twelve to sixteen in one hospital were rape victims. Often the rape was committed by a father, stepfather, or other close relative. In Costa Rica, 95 percent of pregnant clients under fifteen years of age at a hospital were victims of incest.

"Bride-burning" is not uncommon in India, where official police records show 4,835 women were killed in 1990 because their families failed to meet demands for money promised in the dowry. In greater Bombay, one of every five deaths among women aged fifteen to forty-four was reported to be "accidental burns."

Women are at the greatest risk of abuse in their homes and at the hands of men they know. At a police station in São Paulo, Brazil, 70 percent of all reported cases of violence against women took place in the home. In Santiago, Chile, three quarters of assault-related injuries to women were caused by family members. In Canada, 62 percent of women murdered in 1987 died at the hands of their partners.

Abuse of alcohol and drugs is a factor behind domestic abuse. Economic and social conditions, such as unemployment, poverty, and frustrating work conditions, also lead to gender-based violence. Research also shows that violence is a learned behavior. Today's violent husbands may have been abused themselves as children or have watched their mothers suffer abuse. One study in the United States found that men who saw their parents hurt each other were three times more likely to hit their wives and ten times more likely to attack them with a weapon than those who had grown up in nonviolent homes.[4]

Being There for the Victims

Domestic abuse is no respecter of social or economic class, race, or neighborhood. You can probably assume that there is a victim in your congregation or community. What happens in the church when we discover that there is a victim of domestic violence in our midst? Unfortunately, our track record has not been good.

The United Church of Canada funded a study of the experiences of victims and offenders. It uncovered some ways that victims are failed by the church.

Neglect. The church community is not quick to surround the victim with support. Frequently pastors are reluctant to call, and church members do not offer support. Some denominations do not have a clear stand on domestic violence or helpful resources. Victims have stated that they do not feel a message of concern in church publications, from the pulpit, or within the community.

Scapegoating. Faith communities sometimes freeze out the victims as completely as the offenders. The message is that victims are guilty by association.

Loss of a church community. In despair or anger, neglected victims withdraw from the church.

Some Practical Advice

If you hope to provide shelter or support for someone who is being battered, it is necessary to have some practical guidelines. Linda Johnson Seyenkulo offers some suggestions including the following:[5]

Victims

- If you are being abused, remember that you are not the only person in that situation. Look for help and support. Your pastor is one person who may be helpful. Or look in the phone book under "domestic violence" or "abuse." Keep phone numbers and addresses of support agencies available in case you need them.
- Find help and support from family and friends. It is important not to become isolated.
- The violence is not your fault.
- Make arrangements in case you have to leave your home and your spouse quickly. Gather car keys, checkbook, charge cards, children's supplies, and money.
- Do not leave your children unless you are in immediate danger. Leaving the children makes custody disputes very difficult.

Friends and Supporters

- If you know someone who is abused or suspect that you know someone, be a friend. Don't let that person become isolated. Be available and trustworthy.
- Listen calmly when a person tells you a story of abuse. Consider the safety of the abused person.

"Machismo"

Farmworkers Self-Help, Inc., is an ecumenical agency that provides services through which Mexican immigrant teen mothers can gain strength and support from one another, pursue common goals to better lives for themselves and their babies, learn skills to be able

---

Reflection or Discussion No. 1

1. Recall a time of need in your life when you experienced the support of the church community. What form did this support take? What feelings did you have about the situation?
2. Recall a time when you felt lonely, isolated, or hurt when friends or church members did not come to your support. Why do you believe that the community did not respond to your need? How did you feel at the time?
3. What suggestions do you have for ways that the church community can be more responsive to the needs of victims of violence, particularly domestic violence? If you are doing this study with a group, brainstorm answers to this question, and have someone write down all the ideas that are generated by the group.

to function in the community, and become leaders for other young people.

Margarita Romo works with farmworker women as director of Farmworkers Self-Help, Inc. in Dade City, Florida. Mexican immigrant farmworkers are among the poorest people in the United States. Many speak no English. The teenage pregnancy rate is very high. Many of the young women have little education, inadequate prenatal medical care, terrible working conditions, and poor housing. The women work hard in the fields all day and have little energy left for child care. Romo tells of the young mother too tired and undernourished to nurse her starving baby.

Romo comments, "Machismo. That's the dark side of life for women who work in the fields. We see its violations in child sexual abuse, rape, and sexual slavery. Machismo uses male privilege, power, and control to treat women as servants."

The women suffer terribly at the hands of their husbands and boyfriends who are themselves lacking in pride and dignity. "Men insist on being the 'master' by putting women down, calling them bad names, isolating them, making women do sexual things against their will, and physically attacking them. The rule of machismo hurts everyone in a family."[6]

Tracey's Story

Tracey Thurman is a young woman who helped to bring the issue of domestic violence to the public eye by bringing suit against a police department. After numerous beatings and threats, Tracey took her young child and left her husband. Her husband refused to grant her a divorce and continued to hang around her, threatening several times to kill her. When Tracey called the police to complain about the harassment, they responded that they could not do anything to help because she called on a holiday weekend. This was despite the fact that Tracey had a restraining order.

Several times Tracey called the police. Each time their response was late or nonexistent.

The last time Tracey called, a police officer drove up to her house and sat in the patrol car while watching the beating that was in progress. Tracey was beaten and stabbed twelve times with a knife while the officer watched. The officer finally approached the batterer but made no arrest. He then stood by and watched again as the assailant attacked Tracey again, this time breaking her neck.

Tracey remains partially paralyzed from the attack. Her husband has been convicted of assault.[7]

Roger's Story

Roger had never expected to be a father at the age of nineteen. He had never really thought much about it. When he discovered that his girlfriend Kelly was pregnant, he was surprised but not very concerned. He thought it might be fun to take care of his child sometimes on weekends to give Kelly a break.

When Kelly's parents found out about the pregnancy, however, they were furious and threw her out of the house. Relatives agreed to take Kelly in but did not want a baby around. Soon after the baby was born, Roger found himself doing almost all of the child care. His parents helped him out during the evenings when he was at his job at an all-night grocery store. But in the daytime Roger was on his own with baby Andrea.

Never having spent much time with babies, Roger was surprised by how much Andrea cried. In fact, it seemed to him that she cried all the time. It was difficult for Roger to get any sleep at all during the day, and he often fell asleep at his job.

One morning Roger arrived home from work and fell asleep exhausted on the couch with the baby beside him in her infant seat. She was crying as usual, but Roger was so tired that he fell asleep anyway. A couple of hours later Roger awoke to find Andrea still crying. He tried to get her to take a bottle, but she wouldn't eat. He took her for a walk in the stroller, but she continued to cry. He held her and rocked her, but she still screamed.

Roger tried changing her diaper. When he did, the baby urinated all over his uniform. Angry and frustrated, Roger picked up the baby and shook her hard. She stopped crying. In fact, for the rest of the day, she did not cry and hardly moved at all. She did not eat. She lay in her carrier staring at the ceiling, dozing occasionally. The next day Roger took her to the hospital emergency room where Andrea was diagnosed with a broken neck. Three days later she died.

Uncle Willie's Story

Uncle Willie had always been one of Mark's favorite relatives. He had never married or had any children of his own, but he had always been kind to Mark. There were other relatives, but they all lived in different cities. Mark was the only one close by. When Uncle Willie's memory wandered and he began to need special care, it only seemed natural that he should move in with Mark and his family. After all, they had a large house.

Mark's wife Lois and his teenaged children had never gotten to know Uncle Willie well while he was still young and full of fun. They always though of him as a forgetful old man.

It was difficult for Lois and the children to have a permanent vis-

- One in five women is raped in her lifetime.
- African-American women are almost twice as likely to be raped as white women.
- 78 percent of rapes are committed by relatives, friends, or neighbors.
- Women in the United States are more likely to be assaulted and injured, raped, or killed by a current or former partner than by acquaintances, other family members, and strangers combined.
- Each year 30 percent of the women who are murdered are killed by husbands, boyfriends, or former partners.
- Since 1974, the rates for assault and other crimes against women have increased dramatically, but the rates for the same crimes against men have declined.
- The average prison sentence of men who kill their women partners is two to six years. Women who kill their partners are sentenced on an average of fifteen years, despite the fact that most women who kill do so in self-defense.
- 35 to 40 percent of battered women attempt suicide.
- Wife abuse accounts for 25 percent of suicides by all U.S. women and 50 percent of suicides by African-American women.[8]

—*Marie M. Fortune*

> **Reflection or Discussion No. 2**
>
> 1. Have you ever felt that you might be able to hurt another person or damage property? What were the circumstances?
> 2. Can a person be guilty of violence without actually causing physical harm?
> 3. In the stories of domestic violence, who is guilty of violence?

itor in their home. Amy had to give up her bedroom and move in with her sister so that Uncle Willie could have the room with the bathroom. Mark worked long hours and often traveled for his job, so the bulk of the care fell to Lois and the children.

Uncle Willie sometimes embarrassed them by going out to get the mail or the newspaper wearing only his underwear. He had a habit of going for long walks in the neighborhood and getting lost. Usually a neighbor would bring him home confused and embarrassed. At home Uncle Willie wandered around the house, looking for food or for something to do. Sometimes he soiled the furniture.

Lois found it was easier just to keep him locked in his bedroom. Gradually, she removed all the objects from his room so he wouldn't hurt himself or lose things.

One day, Uncle Willie got out of the house anyway and was gone for a day and a half before being returned home by the police. After that, Lois sometimes strapped him to the bed if she needed to be gone for a long time.

Violence and Sports

Alert sports fans in the United States and Canada have become aware of an ever-lengthening list of professional athletes accused of domestic violence.

The National Football League's 1989 Man of the Year, Warren Moon, admitted to the gathered reporters at a press conference the he had "lost control" and made a "tremendous mistake" in an assault on his wife that led his seven-year-old son to call 911.

The former Boston Celtics player Robert Parish had cultivated a reputation of being a gentleman on and off the court until his former wife revealed the years of abuse she suffered at his hand.

The list of superstars in sports whose names have been linked with violence in the home continues to grow, causing some researchers to examine the link between sports and sexual violence. It appears that the closed, male-only world of professional athletics is dominated with the ethics of aggression, violence, and toughness.

When cases involving celebrities are brought to trial, the judge or jury may be so star-struck that a fair trial is impossible. When multimillionaire baseball player Barry Bonds went to court to request to have his family-support payments cut in half, the judge in charge of the case decided in his favor and then asked for an autograph.

What is the message of this situation in a society where the world of sports provides the heroes for children? Are we giving our tacit approval to violent behavior? Parents and churches face a challenge in passing on a different set of values to our children.

Ideas for Action

1. Adopt a women's shelter or a rape crisis counseling center as a church mission project.
2. Start a support group for victims of abuse.
3. Write letters to members of Congress advocating increased support and protection for victims of domestic crime.
4. Give scholarship help to formerly battered women.
5. Write letters to the editor of your local newspaper.
6. Offer Bible study about women's stories of abuse and of courage in scripture.
7. Plan a program for your congregation or community to help people become aware of the scope of domestic violence.

What other ideas can you add to this list? Create your own list. Then decide how your church can be of help.

The Word of God

There is no longer Jew or Greek, there is no longer slave or free, there is no longer male and female; for all of you are one in Christ Jesus. And if you belong to Christ, then you are Abraham's offspring, heirs according to the promise. (Gal. 3:28–29)

So the LORD God caused a deep sleep to fall upon the man, and he slept; then he took one of his ribs and closed up its place with flesh. And the rib that the LORD God had taken from the man he made into a woman and brought her to the man. Then the man said,

"This at last is bone of my bones
 and flesh of my flesh;
this one shall be called Woman,
 for out of Man this one was taken."

Therefore a man leaves his father and his mother and clings to his wife, and they become one flesh. And the man and his wife were both naked, and were not ashamed. (Gen. 2:21–25)

So then, putting away falsehood, let all of us speak the truth to our neighbors, for we are members of one another. Be angry but do not sin; do not let the sun go down on your anger, and do not make room for the devil. Thieves must give up stealing; rather let them labor and work honestly with their own hands, so as to have something to share with the needy. Let no evil talk come out of your mouths, but only what is useful for building up, as there is need, so that your words may give grace to those who hear. And do not grieve the Holy Spirit of God, with which you were marked with a seal for the day of redemption. Put away from you all bitterness and wrath and anger and wrangling and

---

Reflection or Discussion No. 3

1. How does God intend human beings to live in relationship with one another?
2. The marriage relationship is often used in scripture as a metaphor for the relationship between God and the faithful individual. How does our relationship with God suffer when we abuse family relationships?

slander, together with all malice, and be kind to one another, tenderhearted, forgiving one another as God in Christ has forgiven you. (Eph. 4:25–32)

PRAYER

O God, source of all love and comfort, you desire that we live in loving relationships. Yet in a world torn apart by stress and violence, even our homes have turned into battlegrounds. Send peace into our fractured lives, we pray. Forgive us for hurting the ones we love. Forgive us for abandoning the ones who are hurt. Amen.

CHAPTER FIVE
Violence in the Media

If there is any excellence and if there is anything worthy of praise, think about these things.
                                                    Phil. 4:8b

A WORD AT THE START

TVs, VCRs, MTV, CDs—the alphabet soup of the mass media has become a fact of life in Canada and the United States. Many families have television sets in every room of the house. In fact, there are more homes with television sets than with indoor plumbing. The choices of programming that are available to the viewer continue to expand at a dazzling rate. Our children spend more time in front of the TV than in school or with their families.

The mass media is the voice of our generation. We cannot imagine lives not connected to the "tube." Radio, television, movies, computer networks, and video games form the soundtrack for our lives.

Violence is a theme of the images that bombard us from all angles. How does this barrage affect our attitudes and our actions? How are our children molded by the things they see? These are questions that citizens of our culture need to ask.

Outline for a One-hour Study Session

Prepare for the Session
- Read Chapter 5.
- Keep track of television viewing using the "Violence Grid."

Begin the Session
- Introduce the Session.
- Report on responses to the "Violence Grid" distributed at the end of the previous session.

Develop the Session
- Ask each person to read silently "The Violent Facts," and "A Model for Success."
- Respond to "Reflection and Discussion No. 1."
- Divide the participants into two teams to debate the issue of limiting violence in the media as described in "Activity."
- Lead the "Bible Study."
- Read aloud "Making a Difference."
- Using "Reflection or Discussion No. 3," discuss an appropriate response to violence in the media for you to take, as a group or as individuals.

Conclude the Session
- Read "Confession."
- Meditate silently.
- Read the prayer responsively.

The Violent Facts

U.S. prime-time television geared toward adults offers five violent acts per hour on the average. Sixty percent of prime-time programs regularly contain violent solutions to conflict situations. That sounds like enough violence to satisfy the well-known American taste for gore. However, it is small time compared to children's cartoons with twenty-six violent acts per hour. *Big World, Small Screen*, a report by the American Psychological Association, informs us that by the time the average child graduates from elementary school, she or he will have witnessed at least 8,000 murders and more than 100,000 other assorted acts of violence.

As early as 1976 the American Medical Association had pronounced TV violence to be a threat to the health and welfare of children and of the society. In 1984, two University of Illinois psychologists published their landmark findings about children who watch a lot of violence on television. In a longitudinal study, L. Rowell Huesmann and Leonard Eron found a strong relationship between children who watched a lot of television violence when they were eight and their aggressive behavior at age thirty. Based on these findings, Eron testified before the U. S. Senate that television violence was one of the causes of aggressive behavior, crime, and violence in society.

Big World, Small Screen concluded that television can cause aggressive behavior and cultivate values that promote violence. The task force called for a federal TV policy to protect society.

Brandon Centerwall, with the University of Washington's School of Public Health, found that the introduction of television into the United States, Canada, and South Africa paralleled increases in the murder rate of each country.

"Taste is not only a part and an index of morality—it is the only morality. The first, and last, and closest trial question to any living creature is, 'What do you like?' Tell me what you like, and I'll tell you what you are," invited John Ruskin, the English literary critic of the nineteenth century. What do our collective tastes say about the North American society today? Increasingly we are a people who enjoy violence. We seek it in our entertainment, our literature, our sports, our language, and our relationships.

Nowhere is our society's obsession with violence so evident as in the mass media. The American Psychological Association warns us that a steady diet of entertainment violence, combined with other factors like unstable families or violence in the neighborhood, can contribute to a tendency to use aggressive or antisocial behavior to deal with problems.

Given our mass culture's current glorification of criminal and violent heroes, is it any wonder that Americans are killing, maiming, raping, and robbing each other at a furious rate—a rate which exceeds that of every other nation that keeps records? According to a March 1991 Senate Judiciary Committee report, the United States is "the most violent and self-destructive nation on earth...."

Mythological interpreter Joseph Campbell observed that since the beginning of civilization, the behavior of every society has been largely molded by its storytellers and myth makers.[1]

Who are the mythmakers of today? Surely the directors and producers of motion pictures must be counted among them. It is on celluloid rather than on paper that the archives of our culture are stored. There have been warrior heroes of every age from King David to Hercules to Superman. However, today's mythical heroes are armed with machine guns and atomic weapons instead of swords and spears.

Michael Medved, film critic for the *New York Post* and cohost of *Sneak Previews*, wrote the bestseller *Hollywood vs. America*. He tells about moviemakers striving for more gruesome and violent effects: "Movie violence is like eating salt. The more you eat, the more you need to eat to taste it at all . . . the death counts have quadrupled, the blast power is increasing by the megaton . . . [audiences] are becoming deaf to it. They've developed an insatiability for raw sensation."

Medved continues by pointing out that one of the most disturbing facets of contemporary violence and a characteristic that distinguishes it from entertainment in former eras is the linking of violence and humor. One twelve-year-old girl commented after viewing the movie *Total Recall*, "I can't say that it's violent, really. It's pretty funny to see people getting shot in the head."

Medved concludes: "Today's movies advance the additional appalling idea that the most appropriate response to the suffering of others is sadistic laughter."[2]

Does the Hollywood creative community have any responsibility for the work that it produces? At least one member of that community believed that it did. Film mogul Harry M. Warner wrote an article for *Christian Science Monitor* in April 1939 in which he pledged "an ever present duty to educate, to stimulate, and demonstrate the fundamentals of free government, free speech, religious tolerance, freedom of press, freedom of assembly, and the greatest possible happiness for the greatest possible number. To that end our company and, I believe, our whole industry, stands pledged—now and for the future."[3]

When characters like Rambo get angry, they blow people away; so children have learned that violence is the way to solve problems.
—*Deborah Prothrow-Stith*, M.D.

[Studies] support the conclusion that viewing television violence leads to aggression that becomes a lasting part of individual behavior patterns.
—*Big World, Small Screen*

Chapter Five: Violence in the Media

Reflection or Discussion No. 1

1. People involved in the arts and media have struggled to uphold the right of freedom of speech. Do you think there should be any limits placed on what can be shown on television or in the movies?
2. What other ways besides government censorship are there to limit the images of violence that appear in our popular media?

The world has seen a cultural revolution since those early days of the movie industry. Almost everyone agrees that popular entertainment has become violent, vulgar, and out of control. It's just that no one can agree on what to do about it.

"We must hold Hollywood and the entire entertainment industry accountable for putting profit ahead of common decency," accused U. S. Senator and presidential candidate Robert Dole in 1995, setting off new debates on the respective roles of the government, the entertainment industry, and the consumers in limiting the overwhelming volume of objectionable material to come out of the popular media.

The Canadian Charter of Rights and Freedoms guarantees the "freedom of thought, belief, opinion and expression, including freedom of the press and other media of communication." The first amendment of the United States Constitution echoes the same viewpoint: "Congress shall make no law . . . abridging the freedom of speech, or of the press."

These are freedoms that North Americans hold dear. Any attempts to place governmental limits on our freedom of expression, even for our own good, is greeted with resistance. Does that mean that there can be no control over the media? Consumers blame producers for presenting a steady diet of violence and vulgarity. Producers blame writers and directors. The writers and directors claim that they are simply producing what the public wants to see. A climate of blame and irresponsibility thrives. Meanwhile parents feel overwhelmed, and children continue to be bombarded with inappropriate images.

A Model for Success

Concern about violence on television is an old story. Most people agree that it is a problem, but interest groups differ as to how to deal with it. The debate over freedom of speech and censorship continues. Whenever the topic of control is broached, someone is sure to cry, "censorship!" Those chiefly concerned about the situation—parents, educators, broadcasters, advertisers, and the artistic community—seldom come together at the same table. These roadblocks seem to insure that the groups primarily concerned about the issue will remain perpetually in diverse camps.

In Canada in 1989 an event occurred that broke the impasse there. Fourteen students were gunned down at Ecole Polytechnique in Montreal. The brutality shocked the Canadian nation and set into motion a serious look at the links between television and violence by the national television regulating commission, Canadian Radio-television and Telecommunications Commission (CRTC).

At around the same time a thirteen-year-old girl whose sister had been brutally raped and murdered circulated a petition demanding a stop to television violence. In a nation of 27 million people, 1.3 million signatures to her petition testified to the depth of the national concern over television violence.

The resulting efforts to control violence on Canadian TV brought forth three important developments. A coding system was created to specify the violence content of all television programs.

Meanwhile the invention of violence chip (or V-chip) technology allows the television set or channel converter to read the classification code. Owners of a television set with a V-chip can blank out programming they decide is inappropriate. This allows parents to determine what amount of violence is acceptable in their own homes. In addition, the television production industry has agreed to a certain amount of self regulation.

The movement to control violence on Canadian television has made great strides since 1989 and is becoming recognized worldwide as a role model for making changes based on cooperation, not confrontation.

> My favorite strategy is the strategy of making . . . [violence] unpopular as we did with smoking and drunk driving.
> —*Deborah Prothrow-Stith*, M.D.

Bible Study

Finally, beloved, whatever is true, whatever is honorable, whatever is just, whatever is pure, whatever is pleasing, whatever is commendable, if there is any excellence and if there is anything worthy of praise, think about these things. (Phil. 4:8)

1. Make a list of things that are true, honorable, just, pure, pleasing, commendable, excellent, and worthy of praise. If you are doing this study with a group, brainstorm a group list.
2. Make a list of television shows, movies, or music that you believe reflect these same values.
3. Make plans to watch some of these "excellent and commendable" movies together as part of an all-church evening program.
4. Publish your list of recommended movies, TV shows, and music in your church newsletter. Continue to add to the list. Perhaps someone could turn the group recommendations into a monthly newsletter column complete with reviews of current movies.

Ideas for Action

1. For one week, while watching television with your family, use the Violence Grid on page 61 of this book. Fill in a square each time you see an act of violence. You may make copies of this page and ask each family member to keep track of the violence they see and to compare notes at the end of the week.

Chapter Five: Violence in the Media

ACTIVITY

After reading the material in this chapter, have two people or two teams of people debate the issue of what can be done to limit the impact of violence in the media.

Reflection or Discussion No. 2

1. What are some other techniques for dealing with the violence in the media?
2. Examine each of the techniques mentioned above or others suggested by members of your group. What role does each technique have in the life of your own family? What role does each technique have in influencing television programming for the community?
3. Make a covenant with the other people in your study group or with your family to try one or more of the above techniques for saying no to violence in the media.

2. Some churches have challenged their members to turn off their televisions for a certain period of time and substitute other family-oriented activities for television viewing.
3. One couple made an agreement not to watch any movies that contain violence.
4. Examine your own tastes in TV viewing. What is it that you enjoy? How much of a role does violence play in the things you choose to watch?
5. Watch television *with* your children. Have you been assuming that Saturday morning cartoons are appropriate for all age levels? That may not be so.

Making a Difference

Groups of Christians have attempted to influence television programming using a variety of methods.

Economic boycott. In an economic boycott, groups refuse to purchase products manufactured by companies that continue to sponsor television programming that is offensive. This technique is extremely effective, but it requires a long-term commitment by a large group of participants.

Letter-writing campaign. Writing letters to sponsors of programs or to the network broadcasting an objectionable show indicating your disapproval of the program is potentially effective in influencing sponsorship. It is most effective if the letters are personal and come from a large number of people. This is often done in conjunction with an economic boycott.

Turning off the TV. This approach may have the most immediate effect for your own family, but may do little to affect what is available on television.

Supporting alternative programming such as PBS or VISN. Even here it is important to be vigilant because not every program fits the requirements of discerning viewers.

VIOLENCE GRID

Instructions: Keep this sheet close to your television set this week. Make a check in the appropriate square each time you observe one of the violent actions mentioned below. You may make copies of this sheet if you would like to engage family members (especially children) in this survey.

Fight	Gun shot	Murder
Beating	Insulting, angry words	Violence against the earth
Racial insult	Violence against a child	Violence against a spouse or partner

CONFESSION

We as church people need to confess our own roles in contributing to the violence of our society instead of closing our eyes and claiming that we have no part in it. Many Christians throughout history have perpetrated violent acts in the name of faith. Many more have been silent witnesses. We can only make a difference in the violence in our society when we begin by admitting to the violence that is within each of us.

We are fascinated by the cruel world of Jeffrey Dahmer. We crave all the bloody details of the murders of Nicole Simpson and Ron Goldman. Our task in the church begins with confession of our own fascination with violence and the potential for violence that exists within our very own hearts.

(Spend time in quiet meditation while you reflect on the attraction that violence has presented in your own life and on the times you have acted or been tempted to act in violence.)

CLOSING PRAYER

Leader: Creator God, we cannot hide from you. We would like to see ourselves as the innocent bystanders in a violent world. But when we are deeply honest we have to admit that we ourselves are in love with violence. We long to see revenge instead of reconciliation.

Response: Forgive us, O God.

Leader: We cheer when the bad guy is annihilated.

Response: Forgive us, O God.

Leader: We believe that might makes right and that the strong survive.

Response: Forgive us, O God.

Leader: We blame the victims for their plight. We wonder what they have done to deserve to be victims.

Response: Forgive us, O God.

Leader: We love to have power over others. It makes us feel strong and confident and secure.

Response: Forgive us, O God.

Leader: We yearn to be the biggest, the strongest, the mightiest while ignoring the poor and the weak. We forget that you came to us as the servant of all and did not hesitate to wash our feet.

Response: Forgive us, O God, for we have sinned.

All: "Rejoice in the Lord always; again I will say, Rejoice. Let your gentleness be known to everyone. The Lord is near" (Phil. 4:4–5).

CHAPTER SIX
Faith as Hope, Faith as Mandate

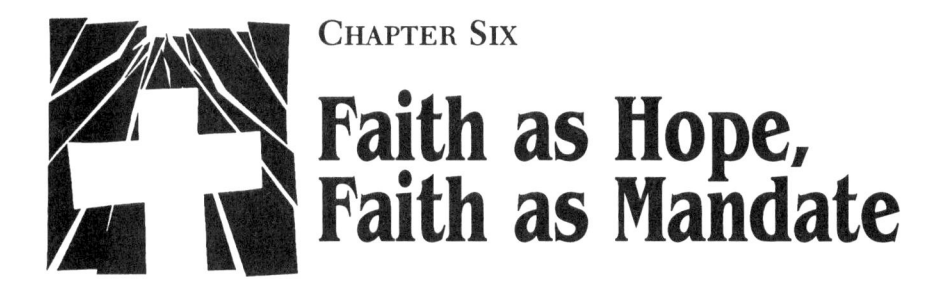

Where there is no vision, the people perish.
Prov. 29:18 (KJV)

A WORD AT THE START

People of faith are gifted with a vision. The book of Revelation promises "a new heaven and a new earth." Isaiah pronounces that "no more shall be heard . . . the sound of weeping and the cry of distress." Violence seems to reign on the earth at this time, but we know that the final chapter has not been written. We know that God plans a different way for people to live together. The vision is a gift with strings attached. It is ours, not to keep, but to share, a gift for the entire world. We are the caretakers of the vision. Our task is to spread the word and to lead the celebration. If the present seems bleak, the future is unimaginably brilliant. That is the gift that Christians have for the world.

We celebrate the hope, but how do we get there from here? The problem of a violent society seems so overwhelming to us because it has so many dimensions. There is a multitude of explanations for the violence that plagues our world. In the same vein, there is no simple solution. The road toward healing must take many turns and detours, and the steps seem small. Socially and politically, some of our greatest conflicts have to do with the route to recovery. Some of those who advocate control over gun ownership are wary of controls on the media. There are those who fight for stricter sentencing of offenders and those who hope for greater emphasis on rehabilitation.

In this chapter you will discover some of the steps that people of faith have taken toward nonviolence. You will make plans to join in the process of healing, and you will celebrate the hope for a future that is in God's hands.

Outline for a One-Hour Study Session

Prepare for the Session
- Read Chapter 6.
- Make plans to dedicate your action plan in context of worship.

Begin the Session
- Introduce Session 6.
- Read aloud "A Word at the Start."
- Ask: "What is hope?" Write responses on newsprint.

Develop the Session
- Read "Turning to Scripture." Address questions in "Reflection or Discussion Nos. 1, 2, 3, and 4."
- Ask volunteers to read aloud "The Power of Hope," including the story of Barbara and John, and use "Reflection or Discussion No. 5."
- Read "What Can the Churches Do?" and use the worksheet activity.
- Read "Churches' Stories."
- Develop a plan of action for your own group or congregation.
- Prepare to dedicate your action plan.

Conclude the Session
- Read the scripture passages.
- Pray the unison prayer.

Turning to Scripture

So, where do we begin to turn things around? First, we seek guidance from scripture. The Old Testament book of Nehemiah has to do with rebuilding. Through Nehemiah's story, we will begin to consider the task of rebuilding the structures that promise safety and security in our own society.

Nehemiah was living in exile in Susa when he received word that the walls of his ancestral city of Jerusalem had been destroyed. "When I heard these words I sat down and wept, and mourned for days, fasting and praying before the God of heaven" (1:4).

Why was this an occasion of mourning for Nehemiah? Walls were an important part of ancient cities. They represented security. Cities were places of refuge to those who lived in outlying towns and villages as well as to the urbanites. The stout walls with their huge fortified gates provided safety.

In the month of Nisan, in the twentieth year of King Artaxerxes, when wine was served him, I carried the wine and gave it to the king. Now, I had never been sad in his presence before. So the king said to me, "Why is your face sad, since you are not sick? This can only be sadness of the heart." Then I was very much afraid. I said to the king, "May the king live forever! Why should my face not be sad, when the city, the place of my ancestors' graves, lies waste, and its gates have been destroyed by fire?"

Then the king said to me, "What do you request?" So I prayed to the God of heaven. Then I said to the king, "If it pleases the king, and if your servant has found favor with you, I ask that you send me to Judah, to the city of my ancestors' graves, so that I may rebuild it." The king said to me (the queen also was sitting beside him), "How long will you be gone, and when will you return?" So it pleased the king to send me, and I set him a date. Then I said to the king, "If it pleases the king, let letters be given me to the governors of the province Beyond the River, that they may grant me passage until I arrive in Judah; and a letter to Asaph, the keeper of the king's forest, directing him to give me timber to make beams for the gates of the temple fortress, and for the wall of the city, and for the house that I shall occupy." And the king granted me what I asked, for the gracious hand of my God was upon me. (Neh. 2:1–8)

Reflection or Discussion No. 1

1. In what ways are we living today in a time when walls of security have been breached? What are some of the "walls" that we have always counted on to provide the security in our lives?
2. What is Nehemiah's first action when he learns that the wall is down? What can we learn from this about beginning our own work of rebuilding?

Reflection or Discussion No. 2

1. What is Nehemiah's plan of action?
2. How does he work with the "authorities"?
3. What can we learn from Nehemiah about creating our own building plan?

Reflection or Discussion No. 3

1. Nehemiah meets opposition to his rebuilding plan. What kinds of opposition can we expect to face in the task of rebuilding our society?
2. Can you think of any "burden bearers" in our society who have to do the work of rebuilding while at the same time carrying the tools for their own security and defense?

Reflection or Discussion No. 4

1. A ceremony of dedication takes place after the wall has been rebuilt. It includes a retelling of the history of God's faithfulness. Why is it important for people to remind themselves of God's faithfulness?
2. How do we do this?

But when Sanballat and Tobiah and the Arabs and the Ammonites and the Ashdodites heard that the repairing of the walls of Jerusalem was going forward and the gaps were beginning to be closed, they were very angry, and all plotted together to come and fight against Jerusalem and to cause confusion in it. So we prayed to our God, and set a guard as a protection against them day and night. . . . From that day on, half of my servants worked on construction, and half held the spears, shields, bows, and body-armor; . . . The burden bearers carried their loads in such a way that each labored on the work with one hand and with the other held a weapon. (Neh. 4:7–17)

Now on the twenty-fourth day of this month the people of Israel were assembled with fasting and in sackcloth, and with earth on their heads. . . . They stood up in their place and read from the book of the law of the LORD their God for a fourth part of the day, and for another fourth they made confession and worshiped the LORD their God. (Neh. 9:1, 3)

The Power of Hope

Research shows that there are some families that manage to nurture strong and healthy children despite poverty, dangerous environments, and other problems.

Sociologist Robert Hill of Morgan State University has identified five factors that allow families to survive and maintain healthy relationships in difficult situations. These factors are

- Strong kinship bonds
- Flexibility of family roles
- Strong spiritual/religious orientation
- Strong work orientation
- High achievement orientation

A report entitled *Caring for Infants and Toddlers in Violent Environments: Hurt, Healing, and Hope* offers a case study to illustrate the point. Barbara lives with her two-year-old son John in a particularly violent neighborhood. Her husband is in prison. "Amidst chronic violence, stress, and trauma, John is thriving. He is bright and cheerful. His mother is not depressed or defeated."

Barbara receives emotional support from family members who live nearby. "In addition, Barbara gains strength from her intense, enduring belief in a better future. She sees the present situation—horrible as it is—as transitional. She looks forward to the day when her husband will return home and when her neighborhood will become a true community."

In the meantime, Barbara works for change in her environment. She participates in welfare-rights activities and led a voter registration drive.[1]

What makes the story of Barbara and John so different from the stories of so many of their neighbors? Barbara has a vision for a future that is new and better than her present life. That is where we who are followers of Christ fit in to the picture. We are bearers of a vision. We are ambassadors of hope.

When we look around us at the need, hope seems a very small gift. The need can be measured in terms of billions of dollars, increased police protection, millions of new job opportunities, educational opportunities, secure housing, adequate medical care, basic societal changes. The list goes on and on, and we end up feeling defeated before we even begin when we focus on the need. Hope seems a very small and intangible thing in the face of so much need.

But in the case of Barbara and her son John and in thousands of other cases, hope makes all the difference in the world. Hope allows a victim of violence and poverty to believe that Barbara can make a difference in her own life and in the lives of others. Hope allows us to see the solutions in place of the needs.

Jerry McAfee is a Baptist preacher who works with gang members. In a sermon he preached at the National Urban Peace and Justice Summit in Kansas City in 1993, he said:

> We are a spiritual people, and anytime we operate outside of that spirituality we're nothing. . . . faith is the substance of things hoped for, and the evidence of things not seen. . . . We see the other side of Jordan, the other side of the Red Sea—and not the circumstances . . . that hinder us from reaching our goal.[2]

Reflection or Discussion No. 5

1. In what ways can people of faith offer hope to a hope-starved world?
2. What unique gifts does the church have to offer to a society torn apart by violence?

Jim Wallis of *Sojourners* magazine describes a conversation he had with some gang members in Watts after the Los Angeles riots: "When asked what the churches could do to help, an 18-year-old gang member looked us straight in the eyes and said: 'We need the churches to lead us to the Lord.'"

Wallis concludes from this experience:

> The escalation of violence on our nation's streets has reached such a crisis that perhaps only the religious community can adequately respond to it. Why? Because the cruel and endemic economic injustice, soul-killing materialism, life-destroying drug traffic, pervasive racism, unprecedented breakdown of family life and structure, and almost total collapse of moral values that have created this culture of violence are, at heart, spiritual issues. . . . We need a change of heart and a change of direction not only among troubled urban youth, but for all of us.[3]

What Can the Churches Do?

Page 69 offers a list of some things that churches can do to make a difference in our violent society. Mark with a ✔ those suggestions that you think have the most potential for making a difference. Mark with a † those items that your church has been involved with. Mark with a ✘ those suggestions that have the most interest for you personally.

What Churches Can Do

_____1. Start an after-school program for children and youth in your community. Provide recreational opportunities, tutoring, and Christian education. Volunteer your time to help out. Provide a safe place for kids to be in the evening.

_____2. Provide a haven for battered women and their children. Help them to get counseling, job training, and legal help.

_____3. Offer parenting courses for adults and teenagers. Include conflict resolution skills in the curriculum.

_____4. Lobby for the restriction of the sale of violent pornography in your community.

_____5. Adopt a gang! Provide alternative programs and evangelism for inner city youth.

_____6. Commission missionaries to serve as advocates for African-American and Latino juveniles in the courts to work with probation officers, law enforcement officials, and youth street workers to assist at-risk youth and their families.

_____7. Sponsor a literacy program to tutor adults and young people in reading skills using trained volunteer tutors.

_____8. Initiate a neighborhood crime-watch program in the area surrounding your church. Suburban churches can work in partnership with inner city churches to help where support is needed.

_____9. Support community-based and minority-owned economic development concerns in doing church business.

_____10. Participate in a prison ministry that offers counseling, rehabilitation, Bible study, literacy programs, worship, or legal help to current or former prisoners.

_____11. Minister to the families of prison inmates. Families, particularly children, of prisoners are the hidden victims of incarceration. Prisoners that maintain close family ties during their imprisonment are far less likely to return to a life of crime.

_____12. Support the victims of crime. These people may feel twice victimized: once by the victimizer and again by an insensitive criminal justice system and a judgmental society.

_____13. Provide ongoing prayer support for victims of violence and injustice.

Based on the interests of church members, congregational resources, and community needs, develop a long-range plan for your church's involvement in stopping violence in your community.

Stop the Violence

The Reverend Jerry Cunningham, senior associate in the Division of Homeland Ministries, Christian Church (Disciples of Christ), presents a list of *110 Things Congregations Can Do to STOP the Violence*.[4] His ideas include the following:

- Use the church facilities to provide alternative programs for children and youth.
- Recruit help from persons from the congregation who work in areas of counseling, law enforcement, health, education, and public policy.
- Cooperate with other congregations to create summer enrichment programs.
- Set up programs in churches for recovery and re-entry of prisoners into society.
- Increase cultural awareness.
- Create a job placement center in the church.
- Support "stay in school" efforts.
- Address the issue of suicide.
- Encourage neighbors to get to know each other and each other's children.
- Create Bible study related to forgiveness, hope, and healing of persons and neighborhoods.

Churches' Stories

▼ In April of 1995 a bomb exploded in Oklahoma City that destroyed lives and dreams and trust around the world. Church people were among the first to arrive at the scene of the disaster. The downtown Oklahoma City churches opened their doors to victims' families and rescue workers, providing food, counseling, and support. Churches from all over the world sent food and supplies. When much of the food became spoiled in the hot sun and the torrential rains, they sent more. Some churches kept their doors open twenty-four hours a day, offering prayer vigils and counseling services.

Many of the rescue workers who gathered in Oklahoma City came out of a response to God's call to help sisters and brothers in need. Rescue workers needed support, too. It was difficult for them not to feel tremendous anger when they found a child's arm or finger in the debris. Pastors and counselors were constantly available to the workers as well as to the families.

Attendance at Heritage Baptist Church was up 50 percent on the Sunday following the bombing. Other churches reported similar attendance patterns.

The most difficult part of the service at First United Methodist Church, which was damaged in the explosion, was the pastor's request that the congregation pray for the bombers.

The tragedy of the Oklahoma City bombing rocked our world and will continue to do so for years. Yet, from the rubble, many victims and rescue workers discovered a new sense of God's presence and grace in the midst of despair. "Peace and justice is what we're fighting for," asserted the secretary of Holy Angels Catholic Church. "If I lose my faith, I lose everything."

▼ In New York State 65 percent of former prison inmates are eventually reincarcerated. Long prison terms do not seem to do much to convince criminals to change their lives. Parolees leave prison with one set of clothes, a bus ticket to an approved location, and forty dollars in cash. Many have nothing in the way of skills or resources to allow them to participate in a new life that is not based on crime. Many return to home situations and problems that have not changed in their absence.

Because they have discerned a call to minister to those who are in prison, the parishioners of Corpus Christi Roman Catholic Church in Rochester, New York, opened Rogers House, a home for ex-offenders. This refuge of temporary safety offers a place for men and women coming out of prison to make the necessary changes for transition back into society.

Counseling by Rogers House staff begins when prisoners are still in the correctional facilities. Former inmates may choose to reside at Rogers House on their release from prison. They are asked to make a ninety-day commitment to intense twenty-four-hour-a-day supervision, to undergo drug and alcohol rehabilitation if necessary, and to receive career training. The contract they sign specifies that they will participate "honestly and openly" in group counseling. They also agree to attend services at Corpus Christi Church during their first thirty days on parole and then to seek a spiritual support system of their own choosing.

Participants in the Rogers House program help to run a restaurant and bakery where they learn job skills and receive employment experience.

"They drop you out of prison with a $40 check and they expect you to turn your life around. It's not that easy," says Dennis Patterson, an inmate of Rogers House. Patterson first went to jail at the age of sixteen and spent the next eighteen years in and out of prison.

"There was no one in my neighborhood who didn't steal, drink, or party. I was taught to rob. When I got out, I had good intentions but none of the tools. Rogers House gave me the tools and the time to deal with my issues.

"I believe Rogers House saved my life. If I weren't here, I'd be back in prison."[5]

▼ The United Black Christians (UBC), an organization of the United Church of Christ (UCC), is addressing the issue of violence in our society by declaring "The Church as Safe Space."

The stated goal of this program is "to engage the African American UCC churches to collectively embrace a common theme and plan of action to secure the rights of our young to have options other than drugs, gangs, and guns for love, employment, and protection."

> The church is called to be safe space. It is the space where young people and children are no longer named by the culture of violence or nihilism, existing with no meaning, no hope, and no love. Rather the church becomes the free space where they find identity and value, a faith to preserve, the courage to resist oppression, and love which can lift them, motivate them and inspire them to claim and contribute their skills, abilities and talents. In the sanctuary of this environment, they are surrounded and connected to mentors and community where they can be rooted in their history, and gain strength, direction and purpose for the living of their lives and for the building of safe and just communities.[6]

▼ Two teenagers from Montview Presbyterian Church in Denver, Colorado, were concerned about the violence in the world around them. Kendra and Tara wanted to do something more than complain. They developed the "Year of Peace" Commitment and asked members of their congregation to endorse it. Several other churches in their presbytery took up the challenge and distributed it to their members. From there it has spread to other churches and presbyteries. Perhaps members of your congregation will want to adopt the Commitment or adapt it to suit your own situation.

Year of Peace Commitment

in this church and in my life:

1. There will be no violence against any persons; no physical or verbal abuse based on race, creed, gender, or sexual orientation.
2. I will demonstrate respect for children and youth, and validate their concerns, encouraging children and youth who provide positive role models for their peers.
3. There will be protection and consolation for victims of violence.
4. I will oppose the use and glorification of violence in the media and in our culture.
5. There will be a commitment to nonviolent resolution of conflict.
6. I will practice respect and love for the earth and all of God's creation.

By signing this commitment to peace, I pledge to support the youth of this church and the youth of our community by examining my own actions and make every effort to practice nonviolence in my life.

Signed_____

Ideas for Action

Congregations that choose to participate in "The Church as Safe Space" are given some suggestions for a plan of action. Perhaps you would like to try one or more of the following:

1. Dedicate your church as safe space for children and youth. Place a banner outside your church identifying it as safe space for children and young people.

   What kind of a banner would give to your community the message that your church is a safe place? Discuss your ideas. Draw some sketches if possible. Perhaps someone in your congregation can use your ideas to create an actual banner for the outside of your sanctuary.

2. Make a public statement identifying what your church is safe *for* and safe *from*.

   Example:

SAFE FROM	SAFE FOR
violence	tender and tough love
guns	affirmation
drugs	healing
hopelessness	strength
negative thinking	pride in identity

3. Create after-school support programs for children and drop-in support centers for youth focused on self-awareness, personal efficacy, and personal responsibility.

4. Create a "rites of passage program" for children and youth that offers a program in African-American history, spirituality and values, vocation and economics, life and health, manhood and womanhood.

5. Establish tutorial centers after school in church facilities to help youngsters with learning disabilities.[7]

"To return violence for violence does nothing but intensify the existence of violence and evil in the universe. Someone must have sense enough and morality enough to cut off the chains of violence and hate."[8]

—*Martin Luther King*

Reflection or Discussion No. 6

1. What do these situations tell us about the role of the churches in supporting victims of violence?
2. What does your church do to support victims and families?
3. What could you do?

Supporting the Victims

A combination of factors sent me to my pastor when my husband was at his most abusive. It was the first time in over forty years I had asked a minister for help. If she had said, "God only gives us what we can handle" (as a friend of mine was told by her pastor), I would probably not be a believer today. Fortunately, she was sympathetic and helpful; she recommended a therapist and made other useful suggestions. She said two things I'll never forget: "God intends us to be whole," and "You can't make your husband well." The second was especially poignant since I'd always thought his problems were my fault.

My son was accused of molesting his daughter. She was placed in my care. The women of the church have been very supportive and have even helped me with her care. But my pastor has ignored the situation. When I tried to talk to him about it, he changed the subject.

One of every three members of a church or synagogue is a victim/survivor of sexual or domestic violence, according to the Seattle-based Center for the Prevention of Sexual and Domestic Violence. Yet the faith community is often the last place those victims will turn for help.[9]

Preparing a Plan of Action

The stories and activities in this chapter give you some ideas of things that churches can do to make a difference in a violent world. It is important, however, that you come up with some ideas of your own. Create your own list by brainstorming ideas together. Present your list to your church's governing body. Use it to help guide your congregation as they develop an action plan providing alternatives to violence.

Planning for Worship

When you have developed a plan of action for yourself or your congregation to take, you may choose to dedicate this plan in the context of congregational worship. See pages 80–83 for resources for worship planning.

74   Chapter Six: Faith as Hope, Faith as Mandate

CLOSING

1. Read aloud the following statement on hope:

> As Christians we are not in the business of predicting happy endings. We are not optimists, trusting things to get better on their own momentum. But we have hope. We remember the story that new life came out of a death that grew out of love. And we live with hope that far beyond the horizon of our wisdom, a new reality is taking shape that will astound us. We cherish the hope that, although it is shrouded in shadow, dawn is ready to shimmer forth and reveal a new heaven, a new earth.
>
> We are called upon to sow and sustain the fresh green promise of tenacious hope. We can help the birth of hope, joining in prayer with all persons of faith, joining with all people of good will in planning and action to cultivate the personal values and social conditions that build up human community. Witnessing to the biblical truth that all persons are created in God's image, we can develop self-respect and mutual respect. From that base, the strong and complex root system of hope can blossom, attending to the healing of those who have been victimized, and addressing the spiritual, economic, political, and social climate and terrain that have supported violence for so long.[10]

2. Read aloud the following scripture passages:

> I consider that the sufferings of this present time are not worth comparing with the glory about to be revealed to us. For the creation waits with eager longing for the revealing of the children of God; for the creation was subjected to futility, not of its own will but by the will of the one who subjected it, in hope that the creation itself will be set free from its bondage to decay and will obtain the freedom of the glory of the children of God. We know that the whole creation has been groaning in labor pains until now; and not only the creation, but we ourselves, who have the first fruits of the Spirit, groan inwardly while we wait for adoption, the redemption of our bodies. For in hope we were saved. Now hope that is seen is not hope. For who hopes for what is seen? But if we hope for what we do not see, we wait for it with patience. (Rom. 8:18–25)

> For I am about to create new heavens
>> and a new earth;
> the former things shall not be remembered
>> or come to mind.
> But be glad and rejoice forever
>> in what I am creating; . . .
> no more shall the sound of weeping be heard . . .
>> or the cry of distress.
> No more shall there be . . .
>> an infant that lives but a few days,
> or an old person who does not live out a lifetime; . . .
> for like the days of a tree shall the days of my people be,
>> and my chosen shall long enjoy the work of their hands.
> They shall not labor in vain,
>> or bear children for calamity; . . .
> Before they call I will answer,
>> while they are yet speaking I will hear.
> The wolf and the lamb shall feed together,
>> the lion shall eat straw like the ox; . . .
> They shall not hurt or destroy
>> on all my holy mountain,
> says the Lord. (Isa. 65:17–25)

> And now, O Lord, what do I wait for?
>> My hope is in you. (Ps. 39:7)

3. Give each person in the group an opportunity for sharing his or her hopes for a less violent future by completing aloud the following sentence fragment: "I hope . . ."

4. Pray

O God of the future, we lay our future in your hands. You have given us the gift of hope and a vision for a new day without violence. Empower us to take the first steps on the road to that new tomorrow. Be our guide and our vision as we step out boldly into a world that you have created with love. Thank you for each of our fellow travelers. Bless now, we pray, these plans we have made, knowing that our plans are small and finite while yours are eternal and infinite. Help us to remember that apart from you we can do nothing. In the name of our God and Savior. Amen.

Resources

Worship Resources

Scripture

Genesis 1:31a
Genesis 2:21–25
Genesis 6:11–13
Genesis 34
Genesis 38
Leviticus 25:8–18
Numbers 15:27–31
Judges 11
Judges 19
2 Samuel 11:1–12:13
2 Samuel 13
Nehemiah
Psalms 7:16
Psalms 18:1–6
Psalms 22
Psalms 39:7
Psalms 139:13–17
Proverbs 21:7
Isaiah 53:7–12
Isaiah 58:6–12
Isaiah 60–61
Isaiah 65:17–25
Jeremiah 6:13–15
Jeremiah 22:1–17
Ezekiel 7:22–27
Ezekiel 45:9
Micah 6:8–12
Habakkuk 2:2–3
Malachi 2:16
Matthew 5:21–48
Matthew 26:52
Luke 4:16–19
Luke 17:3–4
Luke 23:13–35
Romans 8:18–25
1 Corinthians 12:26
Galatians 3:28–29
Ephesians 2:13–20
Ephesians 4:25–32
Ephesians 5:25–6:4
Philippians 4:4–8
James 5:1–6
1 Peter 2:1–6
Revelation 21:1–4

Calls to Worship

Come, behold the works of God
who makes wars cease to the ends of the earth;
who breaks the bow, and shatters the spear;
who burns the chariots with fire.
    The Lord of hosts is with us.
        God is our refuge and strength.
God was in Christ reconciling the world
and entrusting to us the message of reconciliation.[1]

The world belongs to God,
    the earth and all its people.
How good and how lovely it is
    to live together in unity.
Love and faith come together,
    justice and peace join hands.
If the Lord's disciples keep silent
    these stones would shout aloud.
Lord, open our lips,
    and our mouths shall proclaim Your praise.
Let us worship God.[2]

Prayers

Loving and all-knowing God:
We wish that we knew the things that make for peace.
We long for peace in the world,
    for an end to the hostility
        and suspicion that set one against another.
We confess that we engage in bitter conflict,
    in our families,
           communities,
                and churches.
We shout away or silently write off
    those who disagree with us.
We use words that humiliate,
    and glances that stab.
Restore us to ways of peace:
    to patience,
        forgiveness,
           love.
Make us quick to build others up,
    eager to speak the truth in a spirit of love.
So may peace begin with us.[2]

Loving God,
    You have called us to be one,
        to live in unity and harmony,
        and yet we are divided:
            race from race,
            faith from faith,
            rich from poor,
            old from young,
            neighbor from neighbor.
O Lord, by whose cross all enmity is brought to an end:
    break down the walls that separate us,
        tear down fences of hatred and indifference;
    forgive us the sins that divide us,
        free us from pride and self-seeking,
        overcome our prejudices and fears;
    give us courage to open ourselves to others;
        by the power of Your Spirit,
        make us one.[2]

Lord,
plunge me deep into a sense of sadness
at the pain of my sisters and brothers
    inflicted by war,
        prejudice,
            injustice,
                indifference,
that I may learn again to cry as a child until my tears baptize me
into a person who touches with care
those I now touch in prayer.[5]

✟

All have sinned and come short of the glory of God.
    Father, forgive.
The hatred which divides nation from nation, race from race,
    Father, forgive.
The covetous desires of people and nations to possess what is not their own,
    Father, forgive.
The greed which exploits the labors of human beings, and lays waste the earth,
    Father, forgive.
Our envy of the welfare and happiness of others,
    Father, forgive.
Our indifference to the plight of the homeless and the refugee,
    Father, forgive.
The lust which uses, for ignoble ends, the bodies of men and women,
    Father, forgive.
The pride which leads us to trust in ourselves, and not in You,
    Father, forgive.
    "Be kind to one another, tender-hearted, forgiving one another, as God in Christ forgave you."
May the Almighty God grant us forgiveness of all our sins, and the grace and comfort of the Holy Spirit. Amen.
(This litany is offered every Friday noon in the bombed ruins of Coventry Cathedral, England.)

✟

Creator of all Things,
We look around us with new eyes of wonder and offer everlasting praise for all things good and beautiful: tiny toes of newborn babies, droplets of rain on uncurling blades of grass, the smell of a summer storm.

We thank you for all things strong and brave: the lined faces and the gnarled hands of the old, old women in the park, the proud faces of the young men brave enough to say yes to you and no to the evil of this world.

We cry for all things broken: broken glass and crumbling buildings, broken lives and hopes that have died, birds with broken wings that can not fly away from the dangers of the streets.

We pray for all things new: new life, new hope, new directions, new ways of being a friend, new ways of loving and caring.

✝

O Holy and Eternal God, we are grateful that you have called us your children. The water of new life washes away old ways. Cleanse us. The wind of the Spirit blows fresh and clean. Renew us. We are yours. Use us for new life. Amen.

✝

Unison Prayer after a Tragedy
Eternal God, we acknowledge the uncertainty of our life on earth. Look tenderly upon your people overwhelmed by loss and sorrow. Lighten their darkness with your presence. In their grief, confusion, and anger, help them to find peace.

We pray for all whose lives are touched by tragedy. We pray for the families and friends of those who have died. Strengthen and comfort all care givers and those who will continue to comfort, heal, and rebuild. May those who grieve not walk alone through this valley of the shadow of death.

O God of mercy and of all nations, we acknowledge that you are a God of justice and compassion. We know you call us to work for reconciliation in the name of Jesus Christ. As we confront the terror that comes by day and by night, take away our fear. Put into our hearts in the place of fear a firm resolve to renounce evil and all its powers in the world. Keep us from cynicism, apathy, or despair.

Hear us, O God, whose Son hung on the cross for such sin as this, and who died for us, and who reigns in glory for us. Receive our silent prayers as we pray in the name of Jesus Christ our Risen Lord and Savior.

Resources: Worship Resources

Study Resources

General

Dear, John. *The God of Peace: Toward a Theology of Nonviolence.* Maryknoll, N.Y.: Orbis Books, 1994.

   This work examines the Christian theology of nonviolence through the church's history.

"Violence: Roots, Realities, Redemption," *Church and Society* 85, no. 3. January/February, 1995.

   This issue examines the issue of violence, trying to define violence and to offer a vision for redemption in a society that has become obsessed with violence.

Criminal Justice

A Call to Action: An Analysis and Overview of the United States Criminal Justice System, With Recommendations From the National Commission on Crime and Justice. Chicago: Third World Press, 1993.

   An analysis of the problems of the United States criminal justice system, especially the over-representation of African-American men.

Murray, James M. *Fifty Things You Can Do About Guns.* San Francisco: Robert D. Reed, 1994.

   A guide for ending gun violence in local communities.

Redefining Justice: Crime and Punishment in the Faith Community. American Friends Service Committee, Criminal Justice Program, 1611 Telegraph #1501, Oakland, CA 94612.

   A guide for study and discussion.

Violence in the Media

Beyond Blame: Challenging Violence in the Media. Los Angeles: Center for Media Literacy, 1995. (800–226–9494)

   A comprehensive video-based community education program for educating children, youth, families, and parents about violence in the media. Contains leader's guides, handout masters, video segments, and background resources for use in schools, afterschool programs, youth groups, religious education, and community outreach.

Duckert, Mary. *Who Touched the Remote Control? Television and Christian Choices.* New York: Friendship Press, 1990.

   This resource contains activities for children and adults to link the media to their religious faith.

Fore, William F. *Mythmakers: Gospel Culture and the Media.* New York: Friendship Press, 1991.

    Television, radio, newspapers, magazines, and films present the world to us and determine what world we see. *Mythmakers* invites us to take a close look at our mediated culture, while reminding us that Christians are called to view the world through the lens of the gospel.

Gore, Tipper. *Raising PG Kids in an X-Rated Society.* Nashville: Abingdon Press, 1987.

    An expose of the entertainment industry and a guide to provide children with responsible viewing choices.

Media and Violence, Part One: Making the Connections and *Part Two: Finding the Solutions.* Los Angeles: Center for Media Literacy, 1993. (800–226–9494)

    These two issues of *Media & Values* magazine provide a comprehensive "short course" on the issue of violence in the media. Contains thoughtful articles, research summaries, recommendations for action at home, at church, in the community. Also available in quantity with study/discussion guide for five-session adult or youth education.

Medved, Michael. *Hollywood vs. America.* New York: HarperPerennial, 1992.

    A movie critic discusses the film industry's obsession with violence as well as its attack on religion, the family, and traditional values.

Miller, Mark Crispin, ed. *Seeing Through Movies: A Pantheon Guide to Popular Culture.* New York: Pantheon Books, 1990.

    Six essays explore the ways that movies exert an influence on every aspect of contemporary society.

Peterson, Linda Woods. *The Electronic Lifeline: A Media Exploration for Youth.* New York: Friendship Press, 1990.

    This study guide helps young people make responsible and faithful decisions concerning their use of movies, music, video games, and television.

Pomeroy, Dave. *Video Violence and Values: A Guide to the Use of Video.* New York: Friendship Press, 1990.

    The growing use of violence and sexual violence in videos available for home use leads to an outcry for responsible viewing. This resource offers plans for a four-session seminar to teach parents and church leaders how to make use of videos constructively.

Schultze, Quentin J., et al, Calvin Center for Christian Scholarship. *Dancing in the Dark: Youth, Popular Culture, and the Electronic Media.* Grand Rapids: William B. Eerdmans Publishing Co., 1991.

A team of writers tries to make sense of North American society and culture by studying music, movies, and television.

Domestic Violence

Fortune, Marie M. *Violence in the Family.* Cleveland: Pilgrim Press, 1991.

This resource helps to provide continuing education for clergy and laity in responding to religious questions.

Funk, Rus Ervin. *Stopping Rape: A Challenge for Men.* Philadelphia: New Society Publishers, 1993.

This book provides a discussion aimed at breaking down cultural attitudes that support sexual violence by helping men understand the impact of rape and sexual assault.

Leonard, Joe H., Jr. *Tough Talk: Men Confronting Men Who Abuse,* Louisville: Presbyterian Publishing House.

Messner, Michael A., and Donald F Sabo. *Sex, Violence, and Power in Sports: Rethinking Masculinity.* Freedom, Calif.: The Crossing Press, 1994.

Contains essays that explore behavior and attitudes among male athletes that lead to violence and sexual assault.

"No Punching Judy." Unitarian Universalist Service Committee Operations, Cambridge, Mass.

A video-based religious education curriculum about domestic violence.

"Women and Violence: A Faith Perspective." Justice for Women Working Group of the National Council of Churches, New York.

A reproducible pamphlet including facts, Bible study, and suggestions for churches.

Children and Youth

Canada, Geoffrey. *Fist Stick Knife Gun: A Personal History of Violence in America.* Boston: Beacon Press, 1995.

A personal account of childhood experiences with violence from the author's work with children in New York City.

Daley, Shannon P., and Kathleen A. Guy. *Welcome the Child: A Child Advocacy Guide for Churches.* New York: Friendship Press, 1994.

The world is not safe for children, but it should be! This expanded version of the groundbreaking Children's Defense Fund book teaches how to make a difference in the lives of the most vulnerable of God's children. Factual information about national and global conditions is supplemented with worship and Bible study ideas, worksheets for data-gathering, action plans, resources and suggestions for networking.

Garabino, James, Nancy Dubrow, Kathleen Kostelny, and Carole Pardo. *Children in Danger: Coping with the Consequences of Community Violence.* San Francisco: Jossey Bass Publishers, 1992.

This book looks at the way children's lives are affected by violence, comparing the behaviors of children in Lebanon and Mozambique to those in South Central Los Angeles and Chicago. It offers suggestions for community involvement.

MacDonald, Bonnie Glass. *Surely Heed Their Cry: A Presbyterian Guide to Child Abuse Prevention, Intervention, and Healing.* Presbyterian Church (U.S.A.), 1993.

A guide to child abuse: prevention, intervention, and healing. It includes study questions, resource lists, and suggestions for ministry.

Prothrow-Stith, Deborah. *Deadly Consequences: How Violence Is Destroying Our Teenage Population and A Plan to Begin Solving the Problem.* New York: HarperCollins, 1993.

Dr. Prothrow-Stith is a pioneer of the concept that violence is a public health problem and needs to be treated as such. She looks at what she believes are contributing factors to the rise in violence among youth including availability of handguns, lack of hopefulness for the future, and television. She offers a comprehensive solution that involves a broad range of leaders.

The Things That Make for Peace: The Churches' Anti-Violence Action Network. National Council of Churches, Environmental and Economic Justice, 475 Riverside Drive, Room 572, New York, NY 10115.

This action guide is produced by churches in collaboration with street youth. Its goal is to address the problems of crime and violence in young people. It is loaded with action ideas for congregations.

Racial Violence

America's Original Sin: A Study Guide on White Racism. Sojourners Resource Center, Box 29272, Washington, DC 20017.

Nine study sessions are each accompanied by questions to engage participants in a process of repentance, reflection, and action.

Brown, Robert McAfee. *Religion and Violence.* Philadelphia: The Westminster Press, 1973.

Subtitled "A Primer for White Americans," this book is a classic in the field of race relations, violence, and Christianity.

Butterfield, Fox. *All God's Children: The Bosket Family and the American Tradition of Violence.* New York: Alfred A Knopf, 1995.

The book traces the violent history of an African-American family from slavery in the American south through its present situation in the ghettos and jails of New York City.

West, Cornell. *Race Matters.* Boston: Beacon Press, 1993.

Breaking away from traditional liberal and conservative views, West examines the question of race in a new framework.

Criminal Justice

Mackey, Virginia. *Restorative Justice: Toward Nonviolence.* Presbyterian Criminal Justice Program, Presbyterian Church (USA).

The present criminal justice system offers neither justice to the accused nor safety to society. What can a faithful church do about such a situation? This discussion paper offers some ideas.

Wilkinson, Henrietta. *Victims of Crime: A Christian Perspective.* Louisville: Presbyterian Criminal Justice Program, PC(USA).

A discussion of victims' situations, feelings, and needs, with guidelines for pastoral care. Includes study/action guide, 7- and 13-session syllabus, and bibliography.

Devotional Materials

Life in All Its Fullness: The Word of God and Human Rights. New York: American Bible Society, produced for the Human Rights Office, National Council of Churches of Christ in the U.S.A., 1992.

Selected Bible passages that affirm human rights and a study guide.

McAllister, Pam. *Standing in the Need of Prayer: Devotions for Christians in Prison.* Criminal Justice Program, PC(USA).

There is a prayer for each week, a scripture passage for each day, contemporary writings that relate to the theme for the week, questions for thought or discussion, and a closing prayer.

Organizations

Action Group on Violence on Television, Suite 100, 2225 Sheppard Avenue East, Toronto, Ontario, M2J 5C2; (416) 494–8222.
Involved in the attempts to limit violence on Canadian TV.

Canadian Coalition Against Violent Entertainment, 1 Duke Street, Hamilton, Ontario L89 IW9; (416) 524–0508.

Center for Media Literacy, 4727 Wilshire Blvd., #403, Los Angeles, CA 90010; (800) 226–9494; (213) 931–4177; http://websites.earthlink.net/cml. (Formerly Center for Media and Values.)
A nonprofit membership organization spearheading the U.S. media literacy movement in schools, churches, parent, and community groups. Publishes and distributes books, videos, and teaching curricula on media violence, ratings, the v-chip, and other media/society issues.

Center for the Prevention of Sexual and Domestic Violence, 1914 N. 34th St., Ste 105, Seattle, WA 98103.
Works with religious communities on issues of sexual abuse and domestic violence.

Center for Study and Prevention of Violence, University of Colorado at Boulder, Institute of Behavioral Science, Campus Box 442, Boulder, CO 80309; (303) 492–1032.
Collects and evaluates violence-related research.

The Center for Victims of Torture, 717 East River Road, Minneapolis, MN 55455; (612) 626–1400.
A treatment center for torture survivors.

Church Council on Justice and Corrections, 507 Bank St., 2d Floor, Ottawa, Ontario, K2P 1Z5; (613) 563–1688.
An interdenominational organization that attempts to address underlying societal issues that lead to crime and violence.

Fresno Interdenominational Refugee Ministries (FIRM), 1603 E. Shields Ave., Fresno, CA 93704; (209) 227–1388.
The focus is on building relationships between the diverse cultures of Fresno. God's Asian Youth Group offers an alternative to the twenty-five active gangs of Southeast Asian youth in the city.

Interfaith Center on Corporate Responsibility, 475 Riverside Dr., Room 566, New York, NY 10115.

A coalition of Protestant, Roman Catholic, and Jewish organizations committed to merging social values with investment decisions.

Murder Victims' Families for Reconciliation, PO Box 208, Atlantic, VA 23303; (804) 824–0948.

Opposes the death penalty.

Open Circle, 583 Ellice Avenue–R. 301, Winnipeg, MB R3B 1Z7; (204) 772–0726.

This program of the Mennonite Central Committee publishes a letter of support to prisoners, prison staff, volunteers, and supporters.

The Parenting Coalition, c/o ACCESS-Lisa Malone, PO Box 921, Abbeville, SC 29260; (803) 459–4661.

Produces *STOP Domestic Violence* a "life-altering holistic learning program for abusers" that focuses on body, mind, emotion, and spirit.

The Churches' Anti-Violence Network, National Council of the Churches of Christ in the U.S.A., Environmental and Economic Justice, 475 Riverside Drive, Room 572, New York, NY 10115; (212) 870–2385.

An ecumenical network in collaboration with street youth and actively involved in addressing the issues of youth and violence in urban America.

Unitarian Universalists Acting to Stop Violence Against Women, 3221 Snyder Avenue, Modesto, CA 95356; (209) 545–2665.

Produces resources and offers support to abused women and congregations seeking to provide help.

Unitarian Universalists for Juvenile Justice, 331 E. Broadmor Drive, Tempe, AZ 85282; (602) 894–6733.

Helps congregations find their way through the juvenile justice system.

Violence Policy Center, 1834 18th St. NW, Washington DC 20009; (202) 822–8200.

A national educational organization that conducts research on violence in America and works to develop violence reduction policies and proposals.

Videography

NOTE: All resources listed below are 1/2" VHS format unless otherwise noted.

Primary Resource

Christian Faith in a Violent World (1996) 28:00; sale: $29.95; rental: $15.00. **Available for sale only from Friendship Press Distribution Office, P.O. Box 37844, Cincinnati, OH 45222-0844 (513) 948-8733. Available for rental only from EcuFILM, 810 Twelfth Ave. S., Nashville, TN 37203 (800) 251-4091 or (615) 242-6277.**

How are Christians called to respond to the violence in our world and thus bring a message of hope? Can Christians repent of the violence *they* perpetrate? This video explores how we as Christians minister to God's word within a violent society by showing three examples of faithful Christians who are working to effect positive change. In this process, the video looks at forms of domestic violence, violence against children, crime, and violence in the media. Throughout each segment these questions are posed and answered: what can the churches do? what can I as an individual do? what gifts and strengths do Christians have that they can use to bring hope into the seemingly hopeless environment of violence? Study guide included.

Secondary Resources

After Sexual Abuse (1992) 52:00; sale: $25.00; rental: free loan (return shipping costs). **Available from Mennonite Central Committee, 21 South 12th St., PO Box 500, Akron, PA 17501-0500 (717) 859-1151 or (717) 859-3889; or 134 Plaza Drive, Winnipeg, MB R3T 5K9.**

Vicki Dyck, a storyteller from Saskatchewan, tells two stories about an incest survivor's struggles to deal with her abuse. The first story, "Seeking the Lord," looks at how an incest survivor comes to a new understanding of God, who failed to protect her; the second, "Learning to Leave," looks anew at biblical teachings on forgiveness. Through these stories the survivor learns to accept that it was "not my fault, but she must also deal with her anger at God who allowed this to happen. This is difficult and sensitive material, and the leader will need to be able to accept the emotions that are triggered. A discussion guide and other study materials are included.

Beyond the News; sale: $69.95 (all four); $19.95 (each). (NOTE: these are special prices for Friendship Press users of this study; please identify yourself that way when ordering). **Available for sale only from: Mennonite Media Ministries, 1251 Virginia Ave., Harrisonburg, VA 22801; (800) 999-3534 or (540) 434-6701.** A series of four videos dealing with violence:

TV Violence and You (1995) 30:00. A probing examination of TV's role in society including the economics of TV and why producers create violence. Media experts Quentin Schultze and George Gerbner, and educator Ramona Pence explain how and by whom our attitudes on race, sex roles, politics, and current events are shaped. Helps to get at root causes of violence. Study guide.

TV Violence and Your Child (1995) 33:00. How should we respond to the violence our children see in the media? Schultze, Gerbner, and Pence again help us learn about the effects of TV violence on our behavior, emotions, and fears. Includes practical tips to lessen the influence of TV in the home. Study guide.

Murder Close Up (1995) 35:00. Features Sister Helen Prejean, whose life was portrayed in the film *Dead Man Walking*. An examination of the question of whether the death penalty is ever right. Does it deter crime? See how the hearts of families of victims have been changed from a desire for revenge to forgiveness. Shows forgiveness as a journey. Study guide.

Firearms Violence (1994) 33:00. Examines the issue of gun control and offers suggestions for responding from a faith perspective. Includes Josh Sugarmann, of the Violence Policy Center, and Felix Sparks, a hunter and former Colorado Supreme Court justice. Study guide.

Broken Vows: Religious Perspectives on Domestic Violence (1994) Part I: 37:00; Part II: 22:00; sale: $139.00 plus shipping and handling; rental: $50.00. **Available from Center for Prevention of Sexual and Domestic Violence, 936 N. 34th St., Ste 200, Seattle, WA 98103 (206) 634-1903.**

Intended for use in study sessions (has an extensive study guide) with clergy, religious educators, and congregations, this video focuses on (1) understanding the dynamics of domestic violence,(2) supporting individuals experiencing domestic violence through the cooperation of religious and secular communities, and (3) developing programs for the prevention of domestic violence. Part I looks at stories of various forms of domestic violence. Part II discusses possible clergy and congregational responses. Includes the Rev. Marie Fortune, Executive Director of the Center for the Prevention of Sexual and Domestic Violence.

Empowering Viewers for Music Videos (1995) 17:00; sale: $15.00. **Available from EcuFilm [see above].**

A depiction of how music videos influence attitudes and behavior—they offer youth a version of the American dream. This video then suggests some guidelines for helping youth navigate through the media world and how to use music videos. Deals with stereotypical images of women and violence perpetrated against them in music videos. A look at media monitoring techniques. Study guide.

Folktales of Peace (1995) 22:00; sale: $20.00; rental: free loan (return shipping costs). **Available from Mennonite Central Committee [see above].**

Storytellers from three different cultures bring these folktales to life: a West Africa woman relates the Limba tale, "Strength"; in "Argument Sticks" a Native American recounts how a resourceful mother helped her sons resolve an argument; "Two Foxes" is an Appalachian tale of deep friendship that foils fussing and fighting. For use with children and in worship. Study guide.

Hear Their Cries: Religious Responses to Child Abuse (1992) 48:00; sale: $129.00 plus shipping and handling; rental: $50.00. **Available from Center for the Prevention of Sexual and Domestic Violence [see above].**

Through stories of individuals and church responses, this video examines the four basic types of child abuse: (1) physical, (2) neglect, (3) emotional, (4) sexual. It also puts forth effective responses in order to protect the child from further abuse, to stop the offender's behavior, and to make religious institutions safe places to seek and find help. An extensive study guide for use in workshop settings.

Non-Violence in a Violent World (1996) 41:00; sale: $60.00 (institutions); $20.00 (individuals); rental: free loan (return shipping costs). **Available from Mennonite Central Committee [see above].**

Five teens, each personally touched by a violent event, frankly share their experiences and feelings with a studio audience of their peers. In a talk-show format, young people ask questions of one another about their Christian commitment to nonviolence as they grapple with today's pervasive violence. A realistic look at today's teenage world. Study guide.

A Roadside View (1992) 15:00; sale: $9.95; rental: $5.00. **Available from American Baptist National Ministries, Box 851, Valley Forge, PA 19482 (800) 222–3872 x 2464.**

After the riots in Los Angeles, several churches played a role in reconciliation. This program from American Baptist Churches highlights that role and shows how to model efforts toward reconciliation across cultures in a highly charged situation. Good discussion starter.

Take Away This Anger (1996) 58:00; sale: $39.95; rental: $20.00 **Available from EcuFilm [see above].**

This documentary, originally seen on ABC and produced by The Episcopal Church for the National Council of Churches, takes a close look at the context of violence in lives of American youth. It also teels the tales of extraordinary efforts by church communities who believe that the way to save our kids is to provide children with the moral compass needed to face a violent world. Examples are from Allentown, Pennsylvania; Los Angeles; and Hillsides, California—with footage also from the *Stand with Children* march in Washington, D.C.

Violence: An American Tradition (1995) 53:00; sale: $99.95; rental: $75.00 (bulk discounts available). **Available from Films for the Humanities and Sciences, PO Box 2053, Princeton, NJ 08543–2053 (800) 257–5126 or (609) 275–1400 x237, fax: (609) 275–3767.**

This HBO special, narrated by Julian Bond, shows how violence is habit-forming and America is addicted. NOTE: This is a *very* strong and graphic documentary, with many stills and shots of violent scenes. From Native Americans as the first victims, to the immigrant experience (frustrated, many turn violent), domestic violence (fueled by alcohol; men who beat their wives also beat their children), child abuse (how authorities ignored what went on in the privacy of the home), this program concludes that we have an historic amnesia about violence—violence is learned; it can be unlearned. Includes analytical comments from Alvin Pouissant, Cornell West, Deborah Prothrow-Stith. Gets at root causes of violence. Powerful, but leader *must* recognize that people can be hurt by the images depicted here.

Violence in the Media (1995) 27:00; sale: $24.95. **Available for *sale* only from EcuFilm [see above].**

This teleconference on violence in the media, with the Rev. Bernard Keels moderating, offers Deborah Prothrow-Stith on research related to media violence, a look at the National Council of Churches' work on media violence creating a climate of fear, and an examination of the Canadian media's violence code. A helpful compendium of good information, especially in relation to the "violence didn't affect me" myth.

Welcoming the Children. (1990) 24:00, Friendship Press.

Designed to be used in conjunction with the study book, *Welcome the Child: A Child Advocacy Guide for Churches,* this video gives local congregations the tools for making a difference for the children both within and beyond their midst. Viewers will see how churches like their own have made a difference for children, working with others to address urgent needs of children through effective approaches that use church resources.

Why We Care: Youth at Risk (1994) 26:30; sale: $29.95; rental: $18.00. **Available from EcuFilm [see above].**

Produced by the United Methodist Board for Global Ministries, this video looks at three locations where faith-empowered people help youth who are at-risk. In Alaska youth in community centers find assistance; in Georgia those victimized by abuse and who are in danger of becoming abusive young adults are helped to get in touch with their lives; in Boston police are shown in community-based programs. A helpful modeling of programs that show positive effects and how the church can work with the community.

Endnotes

CHAPTER 1

1. Jim Wallis, "Worth Fighting For," *Sojourners* 23, no. 2 (Feb/Mar 1994): 10. Reprinted with permission from *Sojourners,* 2401 15th St. NW, Washington, DC 20009; (202) 328–8842; fax (202) 328–8757.
2. "Interview with Deborah Prothrow-Stith," *Alive Now!* 25, no. 1 (January/February 1995): 27.
3. Clifford Krauss, "Mystery of New York, the Suddenly Safer City," *The New York Times* (Sunday, July 23, 1995): section 4: 1 and 4.
4. U.S. Department of Justice, FBI Uniform Crime Report, "Crime in the U.S." (1993).
5. Marie M. Fortune, "Picking Up the Broken Pieces: Responding to Domestic Violence," *Church & Society,* 85, no. 3 (January/February 1995): 44.
6. Marjorie J. Thompson, "Moving Toward Forgiveness," *Presbyterian Survey* 83, no. 2 (March 1993) edited and reprinted from *Weavings: A Journal of the Christian Spiritual Life* 7, no. 2 (March/April 1992). Copyright 1992 by the Upper Room. Used by permission.
7. Lerone Bennett Jr., *What Manner of Man: A Biography of Martin Luther King Jr.* (New York: Pocket Books, Inc., 1965), 64.

CHAPTER 2

1. Jim Wallis, "A Time to Heal, A Time to Build," *Sojourners* 22, no. 7 (August, 1993): 16. Reprinted with permission from *Sojourners,* 2401 15th St. NW, Washington, DC 20009; (202) 328–8842; fax (202) 328–8757.
2. Mac Charles Jones, "Out of the Hog Pen and into Community," *Sojourners* 22, no.7 (August, 1993): 28. Reprinted with permission from *Sojourners,* 2401 15th St. NW, Washington, DC 20009; (202) 328–8842; fax (202) 328–8757.
3. "To Break the Chains of Violence," *The Things That Make for Peace: A Plan of Action,* The Churches' Anti-Violence Action Network, NCCC, 475 Riverside Drive, Room 572, New York, NY 10115.
4. "Cease Fire in the War Against Children," Children's Defense Fund, 25 E. St., NW, Washington, DC 20001.
5. Richard Lacayo, "Law and Order," *Time* 147, no.3 (January 15, 1996): 49–50.

CHAPTER 3

1. Rick Moffat, "Generation Extermination," *This Magazine,* 27 (March 1994): 22–27.
2. Gerard Brandon, "What Do We Really Know About School Violence?" *PSEA Voice for Education,* 26, no. 5 (March 1995): 13.
3. *Ecumenical Networks Corletter* 9, no. 5 (December 1994): 1.
4. Doc Bass, "Tuff Guys Make Tough Transitions: Notes From Operation Break and Build", *The Ecumenical Program for Urban Service* 1, no. 1, (December 1994).
5. "Young Opinions on Violence," *Presbyterian Survey* 82, no. 1 (January/February 1992).
6. Zlata Filipovic, *Zlata's Diary A Child's Life in Sarajevo* (London: Viking, Penguin Books, 1993), 60.
7. Yvonne Delk, "Sanctuary Is More Than Architecture: The Church as Safe Space," *The Things That Make for Peace,* The Churches' Anti-Violence Action Network.
8. Joy D. Osofsky and Emily Fenichel, ed., *Caring for Infants and Toddlers in Violent Environments: Hurt, Healing, and Hope* (Arlington, Va.: The Zero to Three Study Group on Violence, National Center for Clinical Infant Programs, 1994), 4.
9. Kathleen S. Hurty, "Ecu-Letter" *Ecumenical Networks Corletter,* (New York: NCCC) 2.

CHAPTER 4
1. Donna E. Shalala, *Women and Violence: A Faith Perspective* (New York: National Council of Churches, 1994).
2. Ibid.
3. Marie M. Fortune, "Picking up the Broken Pieces: Responding to Domestic Violence," *Church & Society* 85, no. 3 (Jan/Feb 1995): 42–43.
4. "Violence Against Women," *Focus on Women* (New York: United Nations Department of Public Information, DPI/1595/Wom—95-01657—Jan, 1995—30M): 2–3.
5. Adapted from Linda Johnson Seyenkulo, "The Big IFs," *Lutheran Woman Today*, 8, no. 10 (November 1995), 28–31.
6. "Seeing the Bird Fly," *Common Ground* 7 (1993).
7. Fortune, 40–41.
8. Ibid. 37–38.

CHAPTER 5
1. Arthur Kanegis, "New Heroes for a New Age, *Media and Values* (Fall 1993): 7.
2. Michael Medved, *Hollywood vs. America* (New York: Harper Perennial, HarperCollins, 1992), 186, 189, 192.
3. Mark Crispin, ed., *Seeing Through Movies* (New York: Pantheon Books, 1990) 3.

CHAPTER 6
1. Joy D. Osofsky and Emily Fenichel, ed., *Caring for Infants and Toddlers in Violent Environments: Hurt, Healing, and Hope* (Arlington, Va.: The Zero to Three Study Group on Violence, National Center for Clinical Infant Programs, 1994), 11.
2. "Voices of Pain and Hope," *Sojourners* 22, no. 7 (August, 1993): 24-25. Reprinted with permission from *Sojourners,* 2401 15th St. NW, Washington, DC 20009; (202) 328–8842; fax (202) 328–8757.
3. Jim Wallis, "Worth Fighting For," *Sojourners* 23, no. 2 (February/March, 1994): 10. Reprinted with permission from *Sojourners,* 2401 15th St. NW, Washington, DC 20009; (202) 328–8842; fax (202) 328–8757.
4. Jerry Cunningham, *110 Things Congregations Can Do To STOP the Violence,* PO Box 1986, Indianapolis, IN 46203.
5. Michael Wentzel, "Path to Freedom," *Democrat and Chronicle* (July 22, 1995), 1A, 9A.
6. *The Things That Make for Peace* (New York: The Churches' Anti-Violence Network, National Council of Churches of Christ), 11.
7. Ibid., 24–25.
8. Martin Luther King Jr., "Advice for Living," *Ebony,* Feb., 1958, reprinted in "Responding to Violence," *Alive Now!* 25, no. 1 (January/February, 1995): 5.
9. *Violence and Women: A Faith Perspective,* (New York: National Council of Churches, 1994.)
10. Mary Susan Gast, "Hope in the Strongholds of Violence," *Courage in the Struggle for Justice and Peace,* United Church of Christ 9, no. 8 (Dec. 1994/Jan. 1995), 4.

Resources: Worship
1. Jane Parker Huber, ed., *Peacemaking Through Worship Vol. II* (Louisville: Presbyterian Peacemaking Program, PC(USA), 1992).
2. From the *Iona Community Worship Book* (Wild Goose Publications, 1991). Copyright © 1991 Wild Goose Publications, Iona Community, Glasgow G51 #UU, Scotland, UK.
3. Ibid.
4. Ibid.
5. Excerpted from GUERRILLAS OF GRACE, by Ted Loder. Copyright © 1984 by Lura Media, Inc., San Diego, Calif.